Mergers and Acquisitions

Broc Romanek and Cynthia M. Krus

- Fast track route to mastering mergers and acquisitions

- Covers the key areas of M&A, from detailing how to structure different types of transactions to meet varying objectives to the history of M&A activity and the impact of the Internet and other new technologies

- Examples and lessons from some of the world's most successful businesses, including Daimler-Chrysler, Vodaphone-Mannesman and UFJ Bank

- Includes a glossary of key concepts and a comprehensive resources guide

>>EXPRESS EXEC.COM<<

essential management thinking at your fingertips

Copyright © Capstone Publishing 2002

The right of Broc Romanek and Cynthia M. Krus to be identified as the authors of this work has been asserted in accordance with the Copyright, Designs and Patents Act 1988

First published 2002 by
Capstone Publishing (a Wiley company)
8 Newtec Place
Magdalen Road
Oxford OX4 1RE
United Kingdom
http://www.capstoneideas.com

CIP catalogue records for this book are available from the British Library and the US Library of Congress

ISBN 1-84112-339-0

FSC
Mixed Sources
Product group from well-managed
forests and other controlled sources
Cert no. SGS-COC-2953
www.fsc.org
© 1996 Forest Stewardship Council

Substantial discounts on bulk quantities of Capstone books are available to corporations, professional associations and other organizations. Please contact Capstone for more details on +44 (0)1865 798 623 or (fax) +44 (0)1865 240 941 or (e-mail) info@wiley-capstone.co.uk

Contents

Introduction to ExpressExec

ExpressExec is 3 million words of the latest management thinking compiled into 10 modules. Each module contains 10 individual titles forming a comprehensive resource of current business practice written by leading practitioners in their field. From brand management to balanced scorecard, ExpressExec enables you to grasp the key concepts behind each subject and implement the theory immediately. Each of the 100 titles is available in print and electronic formats.

Through the ExpressExec.com Website you will discover that you can access the complete resource in a number of ways:

» printed books or e-books;
» e-content – PDF or XML (for licensed syndication) adding value to an intranet or Internet site;
» a corporate e-learning/knowledge management solution providing a cost-effective platform for developing skills and sharing knowledge within an organization;
» bespoke delivery – tailored solutions to solve your need.

Why not visit www.expressexec.com and register for free key management briefings, a monthly newsletter and interactive skills checklists. Share your ideas about ExpressExec and your thoughts about business today.

Please contact elound@wiley-capstone.co.uk for more information.

Introduction to Mergers and Acquisitions

The introductory chapter sets forth the major thrusts of this informational book.

» Mergers and acquisitions are an essential vehicle for corporate evolution.
» Mergers and acquisitions are propelled by a number of economic, governmental, and cultural factors.
» Mergers and acquisitions have historically occurred in distinct waves.
» There is no more complicated transaction than a merger or acquisition.

Mergers and acquisitions are an essential vehicle for corporate evolution and therefore are an inevitable phenomenon. Merger and acquisition activity reached its highest point at the end of the 1990s and continues at a frenetic pace. During the 1990s, there were tens of thousands of transactions involving aggregate announced values totaling trillions of dollars. Worldwide in 1999 there were 47 announced transactions valued over $10 billion. In 1991, there were only three completed deals valued over $5 billion and none over $10 billion.[1] Even though merger and acquisition activity began to subside in 2001, this appears to be only a momentary pause.

Merger and acquisition activity is being propelled by a number of strategic factors, including competition, rationalization of business, technological revolution, and globalization. There was also a substantial increase in worldwide merger and acquisition activity, especially in Europe. During the 1990s, merger and acquisition activity was driven by liberalization of government restrictions, easing of cross-border cash flows, and advances in technology which facilitated the ability to effect major international and domestic combinations. This led to substantial growth in international cross-border transactions which is still expected to grow significantly.

Merger and acquisition activity has occurred in waves. Currently, it is believed that we are experiencing the final stages of the fifth wave which featured deal volumes that surpassed the previous wave in the 1980s, a decade which represented one of the most intense periods of merger activity in history. The previous waves occurred at the turn of the century, in the 1920s, and at the end of the 1960s. Although these waves were initiated by economic circumstances, it was the decline of the stock market and the resulting illiquidity of the financial market that ended these waves.

The fourth wave was unique compared with the three previous waves. It especially featured the hostile takeover and the corporate raider. The general public perception of the go-go 1980s, however, was depicted in Michael Douglas's portrayal of Gordon Gekko, the corporate raider in the movie *Wall Street* who declared "Greed is Good." In addition, the junk bond market grew into a tool of high finance whereby bidders for corporations obtained access to billions of dollars to finance raids on some of the largest, most well-established corporations. This access to capital markets meant that megamerger deals became a reality. Before the 1980s, larger US companies had little to worry about in preserving their independence. With the advent of the hostile raid, however, they erected formidable defenses against takeover and increasingly called on state governments to pass laws to make hostile acquisitions more difficult.

The 1980s also featured the rapid growth and decline of the leveraged buyout (LBO), the use of capital to finance a buyout of the firm's stock. In an LBO, a public company goes private by purchasing its publicly outstanding shares. This financing technique was popular in the mid-1980s but became a less viable alternative toward the end of the decade, primarily due to the collapse of the junk bond market, which was used by raiders and LBO firms to finance such transactions.

The decline in merger and acquisition activity at the beginning of the 1990s reversed in 1992, when the volume of transactions intensified and the fifth wave began to swell. However, this wave was distinctly different from the one that had preceded it. The deals of the 1990s were not the highly leveraged hostile transactions that were so common in the 1980s. The 1990s featured more strategic mergers that were not motivated by short-term profits or dependent on highly leveraged capital structures, and which used more equity than debt as the stock market boomed.

The 1990s proved to be equally or even more dynamic in terms of companies evolving through upsizing and growth, downsizing, right-sizing, spinoffs, rollups, divestitures, consolidations, and growth; but with different focus on post-closing synergies, operating efficiencies, increases in customer bases, strategic alliances and market share, and access to new technologies.

There are a number of factors that will perpetuate merger and acquisition activity, including:

» availability of capital;
» falling trade barriers;
» technological revolution – the Internet;
» consolidation of the European market – the euro;
» foreign investment into the Asian market;
» innovative instruments, such as tracking stock, contingent value rights, joint ventures, and other methods of effecting a transaction;

» acceptance of hostile transactions in foreign and domestic markets;
» the easing of regulatory restrictions in regulated industries – banking, insurance, etc.; and
» the acceleration of privatization, including telecommunications.

There is no more complicated transaction than a merger or acquisition. The various issues raised are broad and complex, from tax and securities laws to antitrust and corporate laws. The industries affected by this rapid activity are also diverse, from banking and computer software companies to retailing and healthcare firms. It seems that virtually every executive of every major industry faces a buy or sell decision at some point during his or her career.

As we embrace the new millennium and as technologies converge and business and home consumers increase their demands for truly integrated products and services, we are likely to see even greater merger and acquisition activity in the telecommunications, cable, television, and computer industries.

NOTE

1 Thompson Financial Securities Data (January 2000).

What is a Merger or Acquisition?

Successful mergers and acquisitions are neither an art nor a science, but a process. Determining the objectives of the buyer and seller in negotiating and closing the deal is essential. Chapter 2 details the types of mergers and acquisitions and how the process varies based on the objectives of the buyer and of the seller.

» What is a statutory versus a subsidiary merger?
» When is a stock swap versus cash-out merger more appropriate?
» What are the differences in the processes for a merger and an acquisition?
» What is a leveraged buyout?
» How are mergers and acquisitions financed?
» What are the basic documents of mergers and acquisitions?
» How is a merger or acquisition with a pubic company different than with a private company?

Successful mergers and acquisitions are neither an art nor a science but a process. A study of deals that close with both buyer and seller satisfied shows that the deal followed a sequence, a pattern, a series of steps that have been tried and tested. Therefore, the process of determining the objectives of both buyer and seller and negotiating and closing the deal is essential. For example, when a deal is improperly valued, nobody really wins. To be successful, a transaction must be fair and balanced, reflecting the economic and tax needs of both buyers and sellers, and conveying real and durable value to the shareholders of both companies. Achieving this involves a review and analysis of financial statements, a genuine understanding of how the proposed transaction meets the economic objectives of each party, and recognition of the tax and accounting implications of the deal.

A transaction as complex as a merger or acquisition is fraught with potential problems and pitfalls. Many of these problems arise either in preliminary stages, such as forcing the deal that should not really be done; as a result of mistakes, errors, or omissions owing to inadequate, rushed or misleading due diligence; in not properly allocating risks during the negotiation of definitive documents; or because it became a nightmare to integrate the companies after closing.

TYPES OF MERGERS AND ACQUISITIONS

A merger is a combination of two corporations in which only one corporation survives and the merged corporation goes out of existence. In the merger, the buyer assumes the assets and liabilities of the merged company. Sometimes the term statutory merger is used to refer to this type of business transaction. A statutory merger differs from a subsidiary merger, which is a merger of two companies in which the target company becomes a subsidiary or part of a subsidiary of the parent company. In a reverse subsidiary merger, a subsidiary of the buyer is merged into the target. A merger differs from a consolidation, which is a business combination whereby two or more companies join to form an entirely new company. All of the combining companies are dissolved and only the new company continues to operate. In a consolidation, the original companies cease to exist and their stockholders become stockholders in the new company. Despite the differences, the terms merger and consolidation, as is true for many terms in the merger and acquisition field, are used interchangeably. Another term used more commonly in hostile situations is a takeover, but it also may refer to a friendly merger.

An "acquisition" typically refers to one company – the buyer – which purchases the assets or shares of the seller, with the form of payment being either cash, the securities of the buyer, or other assets of value to the seller. In an asset purchase transaction, the assets conveyed by the seller to the buyer become additional assets of the buyer's company, with the hope and expectation that the value of the assets purchased will exceed the price paid over time, thereby enhancing shareholder value as a result of the strategic or financial benefits of the transaction.

MERGERS VS. ASSET ACQUISITIONS

The most common form of merger or acquisition involves purchasing the stock of the merged or acquired company. An alternative to a stock acquisition is to purchase the selling company's assets. In doing so, the buyer can limit its acquisitions to those parts of the firm that coincide with the buyer's needs. If the buyer purchases all the seller's stock, it assumes the seller's liabilities. The change in stock ownership does not free the new owners of the stock from the seller's liabilities. One way a buyer can avoid assuming the seller's liabilities is to buy only the assets rather than the stock of the seller. In cases in which the buyer purchases a substantial portion of the seller's assets, the courts have ruled that the buyer is responsible for the seller's liabilities – known as a *de facto* merger.

In addition, another advantage of an asset acquisition as opposed to a stock acquisition is that the buyer may not have to gain the approval of shareholders. Such approval is required only when the assets of the target are purchased using shares of the buyer and the buyer does not have enough authorization. This is very different from the position of the seller where its shareholders must approve the sale of a substantial amount of the company's assets.

MAJOR DIFFERENCES BETWEEN A STOCK SWAP MERGER AND AN ASSET ACQUISITION

Typically, shareholders do not vote in an asset acquisition. In a merger, the seller's shareholders receive shares of the survivor or cash, and in asset acquisition, the seller receives stock or cash of the buyer. In an asset acquisition, the seller's liabilities may remain with the seller. In a cash-out merger transaction, the buyer does not want the shareholders of the seller to end up holding voting common stock in the buyer. The buyer wants to pay cash for the seller or if cash is not available, to pay the seller's shareholders non-voting investments in the buyer such as debentures or non-voting preferred shares.

MERGER FINANCING

Mergers may be financed in several ways. Transactions may use all cash, all securities, or a combination of cash and securities. Securities transactions may use the stock of the buyer as well as other securities such as debentures. The stock may be common or preferred. They may be registered, meaning they may be freely resold to the public, or they may be restricted, meaning they cannot be offered for public sale.

Stock transactions may offer the seller's shareholders certain tax benefits that cash transactions do not provide. However, securities transactions require the parties to agree on the value of the securities. This may create some uncertainty and may give cash an advantage over securities transactions from a seller's point of view. However, a large cash transaction may require a buyer to incur debt. Although such deals were common in the 1980s, securities transactions were much more common in the 1990s.

Most negotiated transactions have substantial delays between the acquisition agreement and the closing. Some acquisition techniques, such as cash tender offers, minimize time delays; others, such as stock swap mergers, may have delays of over six months. Whenever there is a delay, the pricing issues are more complex, as one party or the other will absorb the consequences of the value changing during the delay.

THE ACQUISITION PROCESS

Most mergers and acquisitions are negotiated in a friendly environment. This process begins when the management of one firm contacts the seller's management, often through the investment bankers. The management of both firms generally keep the respective boards of directors up to date on the progress of negotiations because mergers usually require approval of the board of directors of both entities. Sometimes this process works smoothly and leads to a quick merger agreement, sometimes the process takes months to accomplish. The companies hire lawyers to negotiate and draft the details of the acquisition document and investment bankers to provide valuation estimates and other financial advice. The lawyers and accountants perform a *due diligence* investigation.

Merger approval procedures

Generally, state statutes that authorize mergers and acquisitions require approvals of the boards of directors and possibly the shareholders of the constituent corporations. The statutes that govern the merger will vary widely, especially when a non-US jurisdiction is involved. Once the board of directors of each company reaches an agreement, they adopt a resolution approving the deal. The board must approve the material terms of the transaction, including the price and structure of the transaction. After the board approval, the constituent corporations may submit the deal to the shareholders for approval. Once approval by the requisite shareholders has been gained, the official documents such as the articles of merger must be submitted to the relevant government official to make the merger effective.

The board of directors may choose to form a special committee of the board to evaluate the merger proposal. Directors who might personally profit from the deal should be excluded from the committee. The more complex or involved the transaction is, the more need there is for a committee. This committee also may seek separate legal counsel. This committee and the board in general need to carefully consider all relevant aspects of the transaction. In connection with the board's review, it is common for the board to retain an investment bank to evaluate the transaction price. This e-investment bank may render a fairness opinion in which it states that the offer is in a range that it determines is fair and accurate. The fairness opinion is essential in a public company transaction.

Upon reaching agreeable terms and receiving board approval, the deal is taken to shareholders for approval through a vote. The requisite percentage of the vote is determined either under corporate law or the corporate governance documents such as the articles of incorporation. Following the approval of the shareholders, the appropriate documents are filed and the deal is completed.

Basic acquisition documents

Most acquisitions follow a predictable trail in the execution of the legal documents. The documents also have a predictable structure; however, the level of detail may vary widely from deal to deal. In the preliminary stage, there is generally a *confidentiality agreement* executed by the parties in order to share non-public business information. In addition, there may be a *letter of intent* signed after the parties have arrived at certain preliminary terms. Then, the essential terms of the deal that establish the material terms are contained in the *definitive agreement*.

The confidentiality agreement is usually the first document to be signed by the parties in an acquisition negotiation. A good one defines the categories of confidential information very broadly and obligates the buyer to keep information received from the seller in strict confidence. The agreement often limits who in the employ of the buyer may have access to information. A seller should not give a prospective purchaser sensitive business information until the buyer has signed a confidentiality agreement.

A buyer and seller often enter into a letter of intent at the conclusion of the initial phase of negotiations. The letter identifies the structure of the proposed transaction and summarizes the basic terms, including pricing and conditions to closing. These conditions may include, for example, approvals by government agencies and consents by third parties, and financing arrangements by the buyer. Most letters of intent are non-binding. A letter of intent may help establish the preliminary terms of a transaction and ferret out any deal-breaking terms and conditions. Once the initial terms of the transactions are agreed to, the attention will turn to the definitive legal documents that will memorialize the transaction. The drafting and negotiation of those documents will usually focus on the past history of the seller, the present condition of the business, and a description of the rules of the game for the future. It also describes the nature and scope of the seller's representations and warranties, the terms of indemnification, and the conditions precedent to closing.

Most acquisition agreements follow a basic structure and include sections regarding:

» consideration or exchange – the stock or assets to be acquired, the consideration to be paid and the timetable for the closing;
» representations and warranties of the seller and the buyer;
» covenants for the seller and buyer;
» conditions precedent to the obligations of the parties;
» circumstances under which the agreement may be terminated;
» indemnification provision, including remedies, if appropriate; and
» miscellaneous provisions such as notice.

The major difference between a stock purchase agreement of a private company and an acquisition agreement comes in the basic terms of the exchange, when the buyer is buying certain assets which must be identified. In addition, the agreement must identify any liabilities that the buyer agrees to assume in an asset deal. In many asset acquisitions, the buyer agrees to assume those liabilities ordinary and necessary to the daily operations of the business, but does not assume extraordinary or contingent liabilities.

The Evolution of Merger and Acquisition Activity

Merger and acquisition activity has been relatively constant for more than a century in the United States and has spread worldwide during the past few decades. Chapter 3 examines how the level and type of activity has evolved.

» When did the use of hostile takeovers become accepted by the general corporate community?
» How is merger activity shaping industries on a global scale?

Since the beginning of the industrial economy in the late 1900s, there has been almost continuous merger activity in the United States. The rest of the world has also experienced prolonged merger activity, albeit not with the same intensity until recently. This activity, which dramatically impacts how each industry is shaped, is likely to continue indefinitely.

Most historians believe that there have been five "waves" of mergers, the first four occurring mainly in the United States.[1] The latest "wave" appears to be nearing its end and frequently has been described as the first international merger wave.[2] Although each wave is a product of its own circumstances, they typically arise in strong "bull" markets and fade when the market declines broadly. Each wave has expected – as well as surprising – consequences. Not only does each one permanently reshape one or more particular industries forever, they normally prompt legislatures and regulators to react in an attempt to reduce the level of merger activity – often to no avail. For example, in the United States, the fourth merger wave prompted state legislatures to enact statutes in an effort to prevent hostile takeovers, and the Internal Revenue Service effectively levied tax penalties on companies that used golden parachutes.

FIRST WAVE

Turn of the last century (1893–1907)

During the first wave, which is sometimes called the "merging for monopoly" wave, there were major horizontal mergers in the basic manufacturing and transportation industries. This merger wave was dominated by large steel and railroad mergers that led to a number of enormous trust monopolies (e.g. US Steel, Bethlehem Steel). Other behemoths were created in the telephone, oil, and mining industries, driven by men who are still remembered today: J.P. Morgan, John D. Rockefeller, and Andrew Carnegie. This wave peaked between 1898 and 1902 and gradually died out due to the Panics of 1904 and 1907, and the outbreak of World War I.

New state laws that allowed the formation of holding companies facilitated this consolidation. In fact, the process that J.P. Morgan used to consolidate the railroads, after nearly 200 of them had become insolvent, became known as "Morganization." This process involved having stockholders of an insolvent railroad place their shares in a voting trust that he controlled until the railroad's debt was repaid – an essentially risk-free proposition for him.[3] The landmark consolidation during this first wave was Andrew Carnegie's $1.4 billion combination of 10 companies to form US Steel.

The monopolies created in the first merger wave were possible because companies were not constrained by government regulation. In the US, Congress acted to limit this consolidation with the adoption of the nineteenth-century Interstate Commerce Act and Sherman Antitrust Act, the first antitrust laws that US regulators sought to enforce.

SECOND WAVE

Between the end of World War I and the 1929 stock market crash (1919 to 1929)

After World War I, consolidation in the industries that were the subject of the first wave continued, and more. This consolidation is sometimes called the "merging for oligopoly" wave. For example, more than 8000 mining and manufacturing companies disappeared through mergers or acquisitions during this period. The wave ended with the market crash in 1929 and the Great Depression that followed.

As monopolies and oligopolies tried to grow even after they dominated their industries, vertical integration became common. Of the 100 largest companies, 20% were holding companies. In fact, merely 200 companies owned nearly half of the wealth in the United States. The US stock market rose at an unprecedented rate – the Dow hit 300 in 1928, which was a 500% increase in only three years, before the bottom fell out of the market a year later. The largest US company, General Motors, got its start during the second wave. Founder William Durant went on a merger binge by forming a holding company and broadening the product line by merging and buying many of the components suppliers of automobiles.[4]

THIRD WAVE

End of World War II until the early 1970s (1945 to 1973)

On the heels of post-World War II prosperity, a prolonged merger wave ensued. During this period, which is sometimes called the "conglomerate merger" wave, numerous established US companies embraced the diversified conglomerate paradigm. In addition, entirely new conglomerates were built from the ground, such as International Telephone & Telegraph (ITT), Ling-Temco-Voight (LTV), and Litton Industries.

Diversification became widely accepted because management skills were assumed to be easily transferable among industries. Managers who believed in this philosophy sought to build the largest companies they could. Faced with growing antitrust scrutiny of both horizontal and vertical mergers, companies sought merger partners in other industries to maintain steady growth, which further fueled diversification. A good example of diversification was the homegrown conglomerate ITT. President Harold Geneen's strategic goal was to grow by merger, and ITT merged with nearly 250 companies in the span of a decade, many of them in unrelated businesses. It was only after the stock prices of conglomerate companies crashed in the late 1960s that diversification gradually fell out of favor.

During this third wave, some companies grew into "multinationals" as they expanded beyond territorial borders. Tax incentives, decreasing trade barriers, and falling transportation costs made investment abroad attractive to some US companies. "Pooling of interest" accounting treatment became widely accepted in the US, and this also encouraged companies to grow by acquisition. The merger wave gradually ended in the early 1970s as the Dow Jones Industrial Average fell by more than a third (e.g. the largest conglomerates fell 86%, and computer and technology stocks fell 77%) and a worldwide energy crisis began. This led to tight money for merger activity and a devaluation of the US dollar.

FOURTH WAVE

1980s

The 1980s merger wave probably is more accurately characterized as a "takeover" wave. As the number of hostile takeovers proliferated, they were recognized gradually as an acceptable tool for growing companies. The first hostile takeover was made in 1974 by Morgan Stanley on behalf of Inco seeking to take over ESB. This bid opened the door for the major investment banks to make hostile takeover bids on behalf of raiders. However, hostile takeovers were viewed with disdain during most of this period because corporate raiders, such as Carl Icahn, T. Boone Pickens, and Ronald Perelman, profited handsomely by putting companies into play (i.e. forced them into being a target), sometimes accepting "greenmail" to sell back equity to management, and sometimes taking over a company to break it up and sell its assets. These raiders leveraged limited resources to make millions of dollars for themselves and never really built anything.

In addition to hostile takeovers, junk bond financing and leveraged buyouts became commonplace and were sources of quick – albeit highly leveraged – capital. Investment banker Drexel Burnham Lambert led the charge in using new and controversial financing techniques to facilitate the takeover of companies.

Alongside the takeovers, a number of companies engaged in strategic megamergers that featured the combination of worldwide resources. Increasingly, US companies sought mergers or acquisitions as a response to global competition, such as Amoco and Exxon buying Canadian oil companies. In addition, non-US companies increasingly bought US companies and other cross-border companies as many of the largest companies in the world were formed in countries outside the US. The best example of this was the 1989 United Kingdom's Beecham Group plc's acquisition of SmithKline Beecham Corporation for $16 billion.

In the mid-1980s, takeovers were somewhat slowed by the development of the ultimate takeover device, the poison pill, and eventual judicial acceptance of them. However, even after the stock market crash in October 1987, merger activity continued, and by 1988 there were more than 200 buyout firms with aggregate assets of $30 billion to facilitate takeovers.

The wave ended amid the collapse of the junk bond market, the implosion of Drexel Burnham, and the serious loan portfolio and capital problems faced by commercial banks in the US. In the aftermath of this wave, the market was jarred by the insider trading scandals and excesses that became evident, including the lawsuits brought by the

US government against some of the best-known names in the market such as Ivan Boesky, a well-known arbitrageur, and Michael Milken, the mastermind behind Drexel Burnham Lambert's novel financing techniques.

SIGNATURE TAKEOVER BATTLE

During the fourth wave, the signature takeover battle was the bidding war for RJR Nabisco in 1988. This battle involved a proposed management buyout led by CEO F. Ross Johnson opposed by Kohlberg Kravis Roberts (KKR), a takeover specialist. During the battle, RJR Nabisco's board faced immense pressure and conflicting facts from its own management team, as each detail was widely reported in the media. The result was a $25 billion leveraged buyout by KKR.

FIFTH WAVE

1993 to the present

The current fifth wave appears to be an international one, as many of the most notable mergers have been either entirely outside the United States or have involved a non-US party. Overall, the worldwide volume of transactions rose from $322 billion in 1992 to $3.2 trillion in 2000. The clearest reflection of this trend is the $180 billion Vodafone AirTouch-Mannesmann AG combination, the largest in history. This February 2000 transaction was a hostile takeover by the British giant for the second largest German telecommunications company. It is quite unlikely that future waves will be dominated by US companies as the importance of the US economy shrinks and the market capitalization of US companies diminishes in relation to the rest of the world.

More mergers and acquisitions are cross-border transactions as real growth for many companies can only be accomplished on a global scale. Other factors play a role, such as technological improvements that have led to the linking of many of the major stock markets. There has been worldwide consolidation in many industries, such as the automobile, telecommunications, airlines, and metal industries. In the highly regulated industries, such as banking, the merger activity is mostly domestic, but even this domestic consolidation is often a response to international competition.

Aside from the corporate recognition of the need to grow globally, the primary reason for the increasing level of international combinations is that the legislative and political climate has been quite favorable. In particular, this may be a primary factor for the level of activity in Europe, from the adoption of a single currency (i.e. the euro) and an increasingly linked market to the widespread privatization of government-controlled entities. Many European governments have significantly liberalized longstanding restrictions that had prevented many cross-border deals, and continue to do so. However, there are occasional setbacks, such as the recent rejection by the European Parliament of a European Union Takeover Directive that had been reached after 12 years of negotiation. For more information about global merger activity, see Chapter 5.

Even in the US, some major impediments to mergers and acquisitions activity have been removed recently. For example, the Telecommunications Act of 1996 and the partial repeal of the Glass-Steagall Act have directly caused consolidation in the telecommunications and financial services industries. As the bureaucracy is slowly lifted in the banking, telecommunications, and insurance industries, the pace of merger activity has been breathtaking and unprecedented. Yet some obstacles remain, such as the difficulty of undertaking a hostile takeover in the US banking industry, as exemplified by the unsuccessful attempt in mid-2001 by SunTrust Bank to interfere with the friendly deal between First Union and Wachovia.

In addition to the global nature of this wave, the pace of the fifth wave has been boosted by the communications and technology revolution wrought primarily by the Internet towards the end of the twentieth century. The incredibly high valuations of many of these technology companies enabled them to buy other technology companies to allow them to grow – or to fill in their product line. The biggest technology companies, such as Microsoft and Cisco, regularly bought 10 or more companies each year. Other companies, like AOL, bought "old-economy" companies, like Time-Warner, to create the consummate "clicks and bricks" media company. For more information about the impact of technology on merger activity, see Chapter 4.

With the 10 largest mergers in history having taken place since 1999, the latest wave appears to be the era of the megamerger. As aptly expressed by Professor Bernard Black: "A billion-dollar deal used to be remarkable. But there were almost 200 mergers of this size or greater last year in the US alone."[5] Emboldened by record high stock prices and faced with global competition, many companies feel pressure to grow by merger or acquisition – or wind up being targets themselves.

While European companies have been more willing to use hostile takeovers, such activity in the US has fluctuated. During this merger wave, the considerable appetite for initial public offerings (IPOs) has diminished the need for leveraged buyouts. However, with the recent slowdown in the IPO market, leveraged buyouts are becoming more popular. Even when the number of hostile transactions was relatively small, the fear of hostile activity undoubtedly fostered the "buy or be bought" mentality.

Since the collapse of Internet company stock prices at the beginning of 2000, the merger wave has slowed considerably, although it has not disappeared, as some technology companies are attractive since they are trading at a fraction of their highs. According to Joseph Flom, the legendary partner of the largest law firm in the world (Skadden, Arps, Slate, Meagher & Flom LLP), the fundamental pressures of consolidation, convergence, technology, and globalization will lead to more merger activity, but not at the frantic pace of the past few years. Even though the markets have dropped considerably, he still believes that the fifth merger wave will continue after a pause of several years.[6]

LEARNING POINTS
Evolution of mergers and acquisitions

» Birth of monopolistic trusts in late 1890s in US.
» Move to vertical integration in 1920s as room to grow became limited.
» Pervasive consolidation within industries in 1920s.
» Rise and fall of diversified conglomerates during 1950s, 1960s, and 1970s.
» Birth of "multinational" companies in 1970s.

» Corporate raiders leverage "junk" debt to buy out and dismantle companies in 1980s.

» Maturation of hostile takeovers as credible change of control strategies emerges during 1990s.

» Beginning in 1980s, non-US companies investing in the US.

» Fueled by change wrought by Internet, accelerated pace of merger activity in late 1990s.

» "Megadeals" become commonplace all over the world in late 1990s.

» Global merger and acquisition activity skyrockets, particularly in Europe and Asia, and is likely to surpass US merger activity soon.

NOTES

1 Alexander Groner, *The American Heritage History of American Business and Industry*, American Heritage, 1972; Matthew Josephson, *The Robber Barons: The Great American Capitalists, 1861–1901*, Harcourt Brace, 1962; Ida Tarbell, *History of the Standard Oil Company*, Amereon Ltd, 1993; Joseph F. Wall, *Andrew Carnegie*, University of Pittsburgh Press, 1989.

2 Bernard Black, "Is this the first international merger wave?," *The M&A Lawyer*, July/August 2000.

3 Charles R. Geisst, *Monopolies in America*, Oxford University Press, 2000.

4 Ed Cray, *Chrome Crisis: General Motors and Its Times*, McGraw-Hill, 1980.

5 Bernard Black, "Is this the first international merger wave?," *The M&A Lawyer*, July/August 2000.

6 Joseph H. Flom, "Mergers and acquisitions: the decade in review," *54 U. Miami L. Rev. 753*, July 2000.

The E-Dimension: Impact of the Internet and Other New Technologies

The Internet and other new technologies are forcing companies to re-examine how they operate – and have given birth to numerous new companies. Chapter 4 explores how the "Internet craze" has spurred record merger activity, including:

» how technology companies rely on mergers and acquisitions as an "exit" strategy; and
» how established companies use mergers and acquisitions as a methodology to grow and as a quick and easy way to fill holes in their product lines.

During the past five years, the number of new Internet and other technology companies has exploded. As envisioned by many of their founders, a large number of these companies ultimately get bought. This factor alone has fueled much of the growth of the fifth merger wave, both before – and after – the cooling of the so-called "New Economy." Even if the current merger wave stalls, most commentators believe that technology will continue to be a major factor in future merger waves, as will the intellectual property particularly that underpins this technology.

It is hard to quantify the extent to which technology has altered the shape and scope of mergers and acquisitions. Many of these transactions are unlike any others in history, both from a valuation perspective and the type of assets that are sought. When valuations of "New Economy" technology companies were at unprecedented levels, some of these "start-ups" were able to buy established "bricks and mortar" Fortune 500 companies. On the other hand, more than a few of these established companies paid ungodly sums to purchase companies that barely had revenue and had only dreams of profits – in search of intellectual property that would enable them to remain competitive.

One shocking example is the $165 billion merger of America Online and Time Warner. AOL, a relatively young Internet company, bought the worldwide leader in traditional media services. This mix of new and old companies can be seen throughout the telephone, software, cable, and media industries, and continues to permeate nearly every industry. For example, banking – one of the oldest industries – has been shaken as rapid changes in technology have sparked a significant number of mergers.

INTELLECTUAL PROPERTY AS THE "CROWN JEWEL" OF A TARGET COMPANY

The motivation for most technology company acquisitions is the intellectual property assets held by these companies, such as patents, trademarks, copyrights, and trade secrets.[1] Unlike prior deals that tended to emphasize profits or economies of scale, these acquisitions focus on intangible assets and their potential. As can be expected, intangible asset valuations are challenging because typical financial modeling techniques do not readily apply.

Obtaining Intellectual Property. Due to the importance of intellectual property in these transactions, it is critical that the acquiror obtains complete ownership of the target's intangible assets, or at least acquires the appropriate license to use this intellectual property. The transfer of intellectual property is an essential aspect of the acquisition and should not be treated as a simple transfer of intellectual property rights. Intellectual property asset schedules play a key role in determining the representations and warranties to be included in the transaction agreement. There are regional differences on how this is done. US agreements typically focus more specifically on the identification and scheduling of intellectual property, while European agreements tend to emphasize the representations and warranties of the validity of the intellectual property.

Carefully listing the intellectual property assets is more important in an acquisition agreement than in a share purchase because asset acquirors normally acquire the assets set forth in the transfer agreement, rather than acquiring them by operation of law.

Licensing and taxation alternatives. It is not uncommon for an acquiror to decide to sell its newly acquired intangible assets to a third party and get a license to use the assets as a tax planning measure. For example, the acquiror may place the intangible assets in a holding company and then license the assets for use. Transactions in which the companies are from different countries can generate more complex tax implications. Pre-transaction considerations should address the local and foreign tax issues and consider whether any tax treaties exist among the respective countries.

If intellectual property is split so that some is sold and some is retained, the parties must determine who will maintain "record" title to specific types of intangible assets – and whether the target can license some of the conveyed intellectual property.

Antitrust considerations. The global antitrust regulators have taken a keen interest in the acquisition of intellectual property rights.[2] In the US, Section 7 of the Clayton Act regarding acquisitions of stock or assets whose effect may be to lessen competition substantially or to create a monopoly is particularly relevant to intellectual property transfers. Patent holders have the rights to sell an exclusive interest in a patent without necessarily violating any antitrust laws. In some circumstances, patent acquisitions generate potential antitrust implications.

Antitrust intellectual property issues sometimes can be resolved by granting licenses to competitors to show that competition can occur.

ACQUIROR'S PERSPECTIVE

During the past decade, the most active acquirors have used mergers and acquisitions to routinely gain access to new technologies that then become the next generation of their product offerings. Technology companies, such as Microsoft and Cisco, make dozens of these acquisitions each year. Even companies not in a technology industry have come to rely on technology acquisitions to modernize the way they conduct their operations.

Often, the value of a start-up technology company is its promise of an upcoming breakthrough technological development. One of the most difficult issues facing an acquiror is determining the likelihood of whether that potential development will succeed. Although there can be no certainty of success, an acquiror can better assess the prospect by extensive analysis of the technology, including conducting due diligence.

Evaluation of intellectual property assets

Frequently, the driving force for technology mergers and acquisitions is the intellectual property of the target. In this case the acquiror needs to ensure that it can obtain full rights to the technology, retain key employees and expertise, and perhaps seek the acquisition of a complementary product line or gain access to a particular distribution channel. The primary objectives should be fully laid out up front so that any potential problems can be addressed as soon as possible and there are no last-minute, deal-breaking surprises.

Even before a purchase price is determined, an acquiror should ascertain the extent of the target's ownership of the technology. If the target has entered into licenses with third parties, either exclusive or non-exclusive, the value of the technology can be significantly diminished. Unfortunately, it is not uncommon for a start-up company not to have the formal agreements in place to ensure that it is the owner of intellectual property.

Due diligence of intellectual property

Thorough due diligence is critical in a technology merger or acquisition, both before approaching a potential target and after reaching an agreement with a target. The type and intensity of the due diligence depends on the facts of each transaction. The due diligence process should include consideration of the following.

Verification of chain of title. It is important for acquirors to trace the chain of title for each piece of intellectual property, and how this is done depends on the countries involved. In the US, this can be done by:

» identifying each inventor and developer;
» determining whether these inventors and developers entered into employment, confidentiality, and invention of assignment agreements. These agreements should set forth who owns the intellectual property. If there is any hole in the chain of title, the acquiror should ask the target to take steps to have the inventor assign rights to the company;
» investigating whether the intellectual property assignment was properly recorded, such as a patent or copyright search;
» reviewing each patent to determine its subject matter and the scope of coverage, and reviewing each license to determine whether the licensee has rights to source code, derivative works, or other parts of the technology; and
» conducting a UCC search and reviewing key agreements to determine whether any third parties have security interests in the intellectual property. If a security interest is found, it may be necessary to obtain that party's consent to an assignment.

Employee issues. To evaluate any potential employee-related problems and to try to retain key employees, an acquiror should:

» obtain a list of all target employees;
» review all employment, confidential information, and invention of assignment agreements. Even though each target employee may not be a developer, they should have executed a confidentiality

agreement that stated that all inventions are the property of the employer;

» determine whether the target has had any conflicts with former employees that could impact its ability to assign inventions to the acquiror; and

» find out whether the target has entered into special technology agreements with the key developers.

Representations and warranties. Among other matters, acquirors should consider asking the target to represent and warrant that:

» the schedule of intangible assets is complete and accurate, including disclosure of all licenses, settlement agreements, consent agreements, ongoing litigation, opposition interference, or other actions;

» the target is the rightful owner of the intangible assets;

» no liens or encumbrances exist with respect to the intangible assets;

» the intellectual property does not infringe the rights of a third party; and

» the acquiror is indemnified for the use of the scheduled intellectual property.

Uncover hidden liabilities. Since start-up companies have grown so fast in the Internet age and typically do not have the accounting infrastructure of an established company, it is not uncommon for some liabilities to be inadvertently omitted from their financial statements. Examples of such "hidden" liability situations are when employers mischaracterize the employment of consultants or independent contractors, so that the requisite withholding payments for employees are not made. Another example is estimating the need to prosecute potential infringers of any copyrights and patents, and the time and costs involved. The damages for these types of situation can be mitigated by requiring the target to leave a portion of the purchase price in escrow until each liability has been uncovered and paid, or by including indemnification provisions.

Retaining key employees

Retention of key people can be the most important aspect of a technology acquisition. Their expertise may be critical to further development or deployment of the technologies that were the basis for the acquisition. However, it is these same target employees who have the greatest potential for employment elsewhere.

The acquiror probably needs to take steps to make it more likely that a key person will stay with the new company. These steps may include:

» *Providing noncompensatory incentives.* The acquiror should talk with key employees before signing an acquisition agreement to evaluate whether those employees will agree to stay on. The target should help the acquiror ascertain what motivates the key personnel (i.e. what attracted those employees to the target company and why those employees stayed as long as they did) by outlining any noncompensatory arrangements, such as work environment, responsibility and other fringe benefits. Often, it is these noncompensatory arrangements that play a key role in distinguishing technology employers from each other.

» *Providing compensatory incentives.* Of course, compensation is always important and receiving some equity in the acquiror often is expected. This normally is in the form of stock options. Acquirors may be able to assure key employees that they will honor all prior employment benefits. However, this does not uniformly work since the upside potential of each company is unique and start-ups tend to have much greater potential than more established acquirors. As a result, a new compensatory package likely will be necessary to incentivize these key personnel to remain with the acquiror.

» *Obtaining noncompete agreements.* Acquirors normally are concerned that key personnel will leave to start a new competitor or work for a current competitor. To protect themselves, they should obtain a non-compete agreement with the target's key employees before entering into an acquisition. The key issue here is to confirm that noncompete agreements are enforceable in the target company's jurisdiction. In some jurisdictions, stand-alone noncompete provisions are not enforceable (such as the State of California in the US), but may be enforceable as a part of an acquisition. In addition, a target can draft its employment agreements to provide a potential acquiror with reasonable assurances that its key employees will not leave to join a competitor for a specified period of time.

TARGET'S PERSPECTIVE

Depending on the financial health of the technology company, it may or may not want to be purchased by a more stable and established company. In today's economy, there are many technology companies that are living on fumes and actively seeking a merger partner.[3]

With the Nasdaq stock market down over half from its peak in 2000, and many telecommunications, media, and technology companies down even more, stock mergers are now rare. There are also relatively few cash mergers as the junk bond market has dried up and banks have tightened their lending standards. The uncertainty over the economy has dampened the merger ardor of many would-be acquirors.

"Venture leasing" companies offer specialized solutions for distressed companies by providing financing for innovative technologies. In exchange for the risk involved, the leases tend to be short and have special protective provisions. These companies include Venture-Leasing.com, Leasing Technologies International, Inc. (www.itonthe net.com), and Heller Financial (www.hellerfinancial.com). Although certain institutional investors do not support poison pills, empirical studies show that they help increase stockholder value in a takeover. Studies by J.P. Morgan & Co. and Georgeson & Company Inc. have shown that rights plans provide increased bargaining power that results in higher prices for stockholders. More than 62% of the S&P 500 companies have adopted stockholder rights plans.[4]

Types of takeover protection

Stockholder rights plans (otherwise known as poison pills) work by potentially diluting a hostile bid if that bid exceeds a percentage (typically 10–20%) of the target's stock without first negotiating with the target's board. Rights plans normally provide for the issuance of rights that permit each stockholder (other than the hostile bidder) to purchase target stock at a 50% discount (a "flip-in" feature) and, if the target is acquired, to purchase the acquiror's stock at a 50% discount (a "flip-over" feature). The rights can be redeemed by the target company's board of directors to permit an approved transaction to proceed at any time before the acquiror reaches the threshold.

A rights plan may be adopted before or after receipt of a hostile bid, but it is preferable to have a rights plan in place before a hostile bidder has made a specific proposal. Since some technology companies have stockholders with holdings above the rights plan threshold, the company should grandfather these holders when it drafts the plan.

State corporate law protections – many US state corporation laws contain interested stockholder, control share acquisition, and other takeover restrictions that may also limit the ability of significant minority stockholders to sell their stakes to third parties interested in acquiring the company.

Corporate charter and bylaw provisions – since charter provisions require stockholder approval, they ideally are implemented before going public. In comparison, bylaw provisions can be made without stockholder approval. To avoid a proxy contest that replaces the board, the charter can mandate classified (also known as "staggered") boards of directors so that only a portion of the board is elected at a particular stockholders' meeting. The charter can prevent stockholders from acting by written consent. The bylaws can prevent stockholders from calling special stockholder meetings to consider a hostile transaction and advance notice bylaws can help the target control the timing and process of a hostile proposal.

BEST PRACTICES – MICROSOFT'S ACQUISITION STRATEGY

Microsoft Corporation has used an acquisition policy to fill - or expand – its product line for many years. As of late 1997, it had bought over 60 companies for more than $2.5 billion. In 1997 alone, it made nearly a dozen acquisitions and was the leader in software acquisitions. According to Bill Gates, co-founder and chairman, his acquisition strategy is driven by what he portends for the technology industry. For example, Mr Gates has expressed the fear that infrastructure and hardware will not keep pace with software innovation.[5] As a result, he has made a number of investments in the broadband arena, such as Comcast and Teledesic.

A perfect example of how Microsoft uses acquisitions to expand its product line was the 1997 purchase of WebTV to enter the online broadcasting market. This was on the heels of its 1995 joint venture to create MSNBC, a 24-hour cable news network. Another example is Microsoft's 2001 acquisitions of NCompass Labs and Great Plains Software. These acquisitions enabled Microsoft to obtain Web content management systems to fill "a gaping hole in the company's application portfolio and foster growth for Microsoft Commerce Server 2000" and "spur increased adoption of Commerce Server 2000 as Microsoft battles the likes of BroadVision and Blue Martini in this market."[6]

As can be expected for such a giant, some deals fall through due to antitrust concerns, such as its $2 billion buyout of Intuit in 1995. Since Intuit was Microsoft's primary competitor in the personal finance arena, the US antitrust regulators sued to block the deal and Microsoft decided not to go ahead.

In addition to its acquisitions, Microsoft makes investments in companies that it may eventually decide to purchase. Sizable investments enable it to have the inside track to become the "exit" strategy for these companies should their technology prove worthwhile. For example, in mid-2001, it agreed to buy Ensemble Studios, developer of Microsoft's popular *Age of Empires* strategy game. Ensemble Studios had previously developed games solely with Microsoft but could have worked with other companies. Now, Microsoft is the sole publisher of Ensemble games.

LEARNING POINTS
Intellectual property as the primary motivating factor to acquire technology companies

Acquiror's perspective:

» How to evaluate intellectual property.
» Due diligence issues, such as:
  » verification of chain of title;
  » employee ownership claims of technology;
  » uncovering hidden liabilities.

» Retention of key employee issues, such as:
  » compensatory packages;
  » noncompensatory benefits;
  » noncompete arrangements.

Target's perspective:

» Depends on relative health of target.
» If unhealthy, technology companies often seek buyer and can facilitate due diligence or seek strategic alliance with customers/suppliers/existing investors.
» If healthy, target should consider taking antitakeover measures.

NOTES

1 Judith L. Church, "Intellectual property issues in mergers and acquisitions," *INSIGHTS*, March 2001.

2 Eleanor M. Fox, "Competition law in the new millennium Foreword: mergers, market access and the millennium," Northwestern School of Law, *Journal of International Law & Business*, 20 J. Intl. L. Bus. 203, Winter 2000.

3 Webmergers.com maintains a running tally of how many technology companies are acquired at www.webmergers.com.

4 Jeffrey N. Gordon, "Poison pills and the European case," *University of Miami Law Review*, 54 U. Miami L. Rev. 839, July 2000.

5 Janet Lowe, *Bill Gates Speaks: insight from the world's greatest entrepreneur*, 1998, p. 79.

6 "Microsoft begins ISV spree – NCompass Labs acquisition comes on heels of Great Plains Software deal," *Computer Reseller News*, May 14, 2001, p. 56.

The Global Dimension

The latest merger wave is truly an international one as global regulators and managers increasingly recognize the importance of capitalism. Chapter 5 discusses the factors that should be considered when engaging in a cross-border transaction.

» Do the acquiror's or target's laws apply – and are there laws that might effectively prevent consummation of a transaction?
» Do the companies have differing cultures and customs so that integration is too difficult?

THE CHANGING INTERNATIONAL M&A LANDSCAPE

This is the first merger wave that can truly be called an international one. Many of the more notable transactions have either involved parties entirely outside the United States or have involved at least one non-US party. This is most clearly exemplified by the fact that the largest deal in history, the $180 billion Vodafone-Mannesmann transaction, was between two non-US firms. The worldwide volume of mergers and acquisitions reached $3.2 trillion in 2000 from $322 billion about a decade previously.

Based on the trends in the marketplace, it is quite unlikely that any future waves will be dominated by US companies as they were in the past. The relative importance of the US is in a steady decline based on any number of factors, including economic and capital-raising ones. As a result, the landscape of mergers and acquisitions from an international perspective is changing. Not only is the sheer volume of deals on the rise, but almost every aspect is dramatically evolving – from the viewpoints of the regulators to the corporate strategies employed. From a regulatory perspective, the growth of international transactions has created a greater need for – and has forced some – global harmonization in the legal and accounting areas. With disparate political interests involved, this is no small feat.

Both large and small companies must now think of global competition and cannot merely focus on their neighboring competitors. Without a global perspective, companies often find themselves an unwilling target. As many of the product markets for larger companies become global in scope, they increasingly seek to penetrate local markets through acquisitions or joint ventures. Since global scale is often necessary to boost earnings, many mergers are intended to have worldwide implications. Cross-border merger and acquisition activity has been steadily increasing and is expected to continue for many years. Below is a brief analysis of how it is impacting various regions of the world.

United States

As more US companies engage in operations outside the US, even the most routine merger or acquisition seems to have a transnational component. As US companies realize that many of their brethren are being bought by companies outside the US, they seek to acquire non-US companies to enhance the likelihood that they can compete with these non-US giants in the future. In addition, the globalization of their clients has led to expansion of US investment bankers, accounting, and law firms.

Europe

Even before it received a boost from the use of a single currency in the late 1990s, the number and size of European mergers and acquisitions had climbed gradually. At the beginning of this merger wave, European companies tended to conduct merger activity "in market" (i.e. within the same country). Now, cross-border transactions are quite common within Europe, and European companies increasingly are looking for targets outside Europe. As the pace of European deals continues unabated, some commentators predict that the European level of merger and acquisition activity during 2002 may surpass that of the US.[1]

In Europe, there has been an unprecedented sharp increase in the number of hostile takeovers during the past few years. Historically, hostile takeovers have been politically difficult in most European countries (with the notable exception of Britain). Now these political impediments are falling, as reflected by the mid-2000 European Union Takeovers Directive that was loosely patterned on the takeover-friendly British and US regulatory framework. Although this Directive was rejected by the European parliament due to the objections of a few countries, it reflects the deregulatory attitude of many regulators and should continue to boost the level of deal activity.

Asia

During the past decade, the level of Asian mergers and acquisitions activity has increased steadily. In 1998, the Asian economic crisis caused a blip in this trend, but by 1999 activity had rebounded. As rapid economic growth continues, this activity should grow as regulators recognize that elimination of restrictions on foreign investment is necessary to provide capital for their countries' economies, and as the trend to transition from control by family-owned enterprises to professional managers continues. For more information about changing attitudes toward merger activity in Japan, see the case study below.

Other areas

In 2001, the level of South American mergers and acquisitions activity has fallen, reflecting slower economic recovery and a general unwillingness to encourage foreign acquisitions. Acquisition activity in Australia and Africa is relatively low compared with the rest of the world, mainly as a function of the limited number of sizable companies in those continents.

FACTORS TO CONSIDER IN A CROSS-BORDER TRANSACTION

Although the basic merger or acquisition is the same worldwide, undertaking a cross-border transaction is more complex than those conducted "in market" because of the multiple sets of laws, customs, cultures, currencies, and other factors that impact the process.

How should the transaction be financed?

The financial structure of the transaction might be impacted by which country the target is in. For example, from a valuation perspective, "flowback" can have a negative impact on the acquiror's stock price and cause regulatory problems (i.e. stock "flowing" back to the acquiror's home jurisdiction). Other types of considerations include the change in the nature of the investments held by institutional investors caused by a stock exchange merger – these investors may be compelled under their own investment guidelines to sell newly acquired stock in the acquiror; and the possible change in the tax treatment of dividends that encourages the sale of the stock (e.g. foreign tax credit is useless to US tax-exempt investors).

The following are issues for an acquiror to address when structuring the transaction.

» If the transaction involves issuing stock, will the stock be common or preferred stock, and will the stock be issued directly to the target or to the target's stockholders? Is the acquiror prepared to be subject to the laws of the target's country if it issues stock in the transaction, particularly the financial disclosure laws?

» After issuing stock, how will the acquiror's stockholder base be composed? How many shares are held by cross-border investors? Does the new composition shift stockholder power dramatically? Will any of the new stockholders cause problems?

» If the transaction involves debt, where will the debt be issued, from "in country" or cross-border? What type of debt will be issued – senior, secured, unsecured, or mezzanine?

» If the transaction involves cash, will cash be raised by raising capital in the public markets, and if so, in which market will the stock be issued? If cash financing is obtained in the target's country, can the acquiror comply with any applicable margin requirements, such as those promulgated by the Federal Reserve Board in the US?

How are the customs and cultures of the parties different?

Before contemplating the transaction, the acquiror should be able to express a clear vision of how the target will be operated and funded. This will be necessary to share with the target and its employees and shareholders, as well as with its own shareholders.

Public relations is important in winning the hearts of the target's employees, communities, and shareholders. One cultural issue is whether the target will still be managed "in country," or whether it will be part of a regional center or managed solely from the acquiror's headquarters. Employees worry about overseas managers and communities wonder about loss of jobs. From a financial perspective, investors will want pro forma information to understand how the combined company will operate going forward. This may require disclosure of financial information to which the target's investors are accustomed, but which is new for the acquiror.

How do the applicable laws govern the transaction?

If the transaction is public, such as a tender offer, the parties generally must abide by the law of the country where the offer will be made. In comparison, the parties can choose which law governs if the transaction is private. They can select "ground rules" that are the laws from either of the home countries, or even a third-party country with established merger laws like the US. If two sets of laws are involved, particularly if one is based on a code system and the other is common law, it is common for both the acquiror and target to have two sets of advisors, one from the country of each party. It is also fairly routine for non-US parties to have their own US investment banker and law firm as advisors in a transaction – even if neither party is from the US.

Even if the parties do not use the target's country's laws as the "ground rules," an acquiror must consider the laws of the target in deciding whether to pursue a combination. For example, there could be laws that pose substantial obstacles to consummating a deal, such as restrictions on ownership. There are more than a few instances of cross-border bids that have failed because the target's government blocked the transaction to stop a company from falling into the hands of another country.

The following are issues for an acquiror to address before a deal is struck with a target.

» Will the target insist on "in market" customs, and if so, will these customs be used as a shield to stall or prevent a transaction?
» How difficult will it be to obtain complete financial information? Are there laws that prohibit disclosure or enable the target to share data that are not reliable?
» What is the role of regulators in the target's country? Do they have tools to effectively stall or prevent a transaction, such as requisite governmental approval under exchange control or national security laws? For example, in the US, under the Exon-Florio provisions of the Trade Act, the President of the United States has the power to block the acquisition or to render it void after it has been completed.
» Will the acquisition have to be approved by the target's shareholders, and does the target's country have laws that make this difficult?
» Does the target have subsidiaries or do business in countries other than its home country, such as Canada, Australia, or Germany, that makes the transfer of those subsidiaries difficult so that they will have to be forcibly divested to consummate the deal?

» Is the target or any of its subsidiaries in a heavily regulated industry (e.g. defense contracting, banking, or insurance) that requires regulatory approval, and if so, will the regulatory delays make it appropriate for the acquisition to take the form of a one-step merger (i.e. without an initial tender offer)?

» How will the formal merger or acquisition agreement be drafted? Will it be local to the acquiror or the target, or a US agreement with one of the local laws governing, or a pure US agreement?

What level of due diligence is appropriate?

Due diligence is critical in a cross-border transaction since there is a greater likelihood for undesirable surprises to surface after an agreement has been reached initially. It is important to establish in the formal agreement what type of due diligence is permitted and what the consequences are of finding certain types of surprises.

The acquiror should ensure that it has adequate access to the target's documentation and personnel to facilitate the due diligence process. In addition to access to all financial information, the acquiror should review the target's loan agreements, severance plans, and other employee agreements to see if the target's change in control would impose any previously undisclosed costs or obligations (e.g. constitute an event of default so as to accelerate outstanding indebtedness). Similarly, any other major agreements should be reviewed, such as licensing and joint venture agreements, to determine whether any benefits may be lost due to the pending change in control.

The target's charter and bylaws should be checked to see if they have any peculiar provisions that might make it more difficult for the acquiror to gain full control of the target. For example, the acquiror should determine whether the target has a shareholder rights plan or poison pill, or has a provision that requires a super-majority vote to approve mergers.

Are there any significant antitrust or noncompetition issues?

Although the US generally has the most aggressively enforced antitrust laws in the world, the European Union has become quite aggressive (e.g. blocking the General Electric-Honeywell merger). Overall, more than 70 countries have their own competition laws, and there are a number of regional economic organizations that have competition law frameworks.[2] If the target is involved in operations out of its home country, the acquiror should conduct a review of the relevant antitrust laws. For more information about antitrust laws, see Chapter 6.

Even if a significant antitrust problem is not present, it may be necessary to report the acquisition in advance to a governmental agency. In the US, the Hart-Scott-Rodino Antitrust Improvements Act requires a notice and waiting period unless the transaction is below specified minimal levels.[3]

The following are issues for an acquiror to address before pursuing a target.

» To what extent do the acquiror and target compete in a line of business?
» Will the acquisition substantially lessen competition in any line of business in any particular country?
» What products or services does the acquiror sell to the target now, or vice versa?

Are there any significant tax or currency issues?

The acquiror should structure the transaction with a complete understanding of the tax implications. This requires an analysis of the interplay of local law and tax treaties as well as the expectation of where future revenues and deductions will be derived. Based on the acquiror's own tax preferences, it may desire current income (i.e. dividends) or capital gain, and should structure the transaction accordingly.

The acquiror must also take care to consider the volatility of any currencies that are implicated in the transaction and ensure that it has adequate protection from downward swings in them before the transaction is closed. If it cannot tolerate the currency risk that is involved in the target's operations, the acquiror should consider the ongoing impact of a volatile currency after the transaction is complete.

CASE STUDY: MERGER ACTIVITY IN JAPAN

Due to a number of factors, mergers – even friendly mergers – have long been frowned upon in Japan. These factors included an inhibitive regulatory environment, poor accounting practices, and the lack of readily available information on companies that might be acquired. Probably the biggest deterrent has been the unique nature of the relationships between boards of directors, shareholders, managers, and employees, as well as the practice of cross-shareholding.

Based on this unique web of cross-shareholding relationships, huge Japanese banks effectively have allowed managers to work free from the pressures of profitability because companies normally place sizable blocks of shares in the hands of these banks and other large institutions in a reciprocal arrangement. These corporate groups, which also bail each other out with loans with favorable terms, are known as "keiretsu." Under these arrangements, it is difficult for activist shareholders to obtain any shareholding clout to pressure management to make any changes, and nearly impossible to conduct a hostile takeover.

Recognizing that such practices were risky after the drop in Japan's equity and real estate markets in the 1980s, when banks were saddled with huge portfolios of non-performing loans, Japan has begun to undergo a number of reforms so that mergers – and foreign investment in general – are more acceptable. For example, market-to-market accounting regulations based on internationally accepted accounting standards were adopted in 2001. Another example was the removal of the ban on pure holding companies in 1997. Now, the Japanese have holding company structures that make it easier for companies to spin off parts of their operations for future sales. As a result, Japanese merger and acquisition activity has increased substantially during the past several years – from $19 billion in 1998 to $100 billion in 2000. This activity is expected to continue – and even increase – as Japan plays catch-up as its old insulated corporate governance framework breaks down.

LEARNING POINTS

Factors to consider in a cross-border transaction:

- » alternative financing methods for a transaction;
- » differing customs and cultures of the parties;
- » differing applicable laws governing the transaction;
- » due diligence practices;
- » antitrust and noncompetition issues; and
- » tax and currency issues.

NOTES

1 Joseph H. Flom, "Mergers & Acquisitions: the decade in review," 54 U. *Miami L. Rev.* 753, July 2000.

2 William M. Hannay, "Transnational competition law aspects of mergers and acquisitions," *Northwestern Journal of International Law & Business*, 20 J. Intl. L. Bus. 287, Winter 2000.

3 16 CFR §802.9. Like the US's HSR Act, the EU's merger policy requires parties to transactions above a certain size threshold to notify the regulator prior to completing the merger or acquisition. In the US, the merging parties must refrain from closing until expiration of a 30-day waiting period. In Europe, a notifiable "concentration" (i.e. a merger, acquisition, or other consolidation) of two or more "undertakings" (i.e. corporations or other entities) must not be implemented until it has been authorized. The EU Commission, however, must decide whether to authorize the transaction within a month.

The State of the Art

Although merger and acquisition activity is relatively constant, the variables involved constantly evolve. Chapter 6 explores the macro- and micro-factors that impact the level and type of this activity, including:

» deregulatory trends;
» market economics;
» performance measures; and
» management incentives.

As could be expected, there are numerous, constantly changing factors that contribute to the cycles of merger and acquisition activity. Some of these factors are macro in nature. For example, consolidation within an industry can be politically motivated and encouraged through regulatory change. Similarly, merger activity is influenced by broad market, economic, and competitive conditions. Today, the impact of these factors changes as their relative importance shifts on a global scale.

Even though the importance of each macro-factor varies depending on the circumstances of a particular transaction, these factors typically are beyond the ability of a company to control. In comparison, companies often can influence the micro-factors and they can play a dominant role in explaining why two companies want to merge at a particular moment in time. These factors typically include the composition and ambitions of the management teams and the financial and stock performance of both companies. The relevance of some of these factors has not changed much over the past decade. Some are debated solely in certain areas of the world and are well established in others. Others are the subject of intense research and neverending debate. For example, the following basic questions are still unanswered and likely to be unknown for some time to come:

» Can mergers and acquisitions be beneficial to the future performance of a particular type of company?
» Are mergers and acquisitions beneficial to the overall economy?
» Will management act in the best interests of shareholders when a company is faced with the likelihood of being "in play?"
» Do mergers and acquisitions improve shareholder wealth? Which shareholders should be considered in answering this question? Short-term? Long-term? Tax-exempt?
» Should the impact of a transaction on a company's employees or community be taken into account when management is deciding whether to accept a takeover bid?

Many commentators argue that most mergers are not beneficial to acquirors in the long run. They posit that the egos of management – as well as the misheld belief that a deal will not fail – still lead companies to seek growth by merger. There are numerous critics of these commentators who believe that the basis for their position is on misguided financial analysis and note the lack of information as to how the acquiror would have fared if the acquisition had not taken place. Some of these critics distinguish negotiated strategic mergers that tend to be more successful than hostile takeovers. They note that hostile takeovers entail a greater likelihood of culture clash if a deal is not friendly because it often leads to performance problems.[1]

MACRO-FACTORS

Regulatory, political, and market change is inevitable and greatly influences general merger and acquisition trends, as well as such trends within particular industries. Most regulatory and political changes are reactionary to past merger and acquisition activity. Market changes appear to be more dependent on myriad factors that are not necessarily tied to merger and acquisition activity. Overall, all of these changes are cyclical, although each may be on a cycle all its own.

Regulatory factors

Deregulation is occurring on a global scale as more countries seek to foster market capitalism. This is best reflected by the record levels of privatization of state-controlled companies, particularly telecommunications companies. After privatization, these newly formed giants have the resources to engage in a string of acquisitions. In addition, many countries are easing restrictions on cross-border mergers as trade barriers continue to fall. Although ultimately rejected by the European Parliament, in mid-2000 the European Union attempted to adopt a Takeover Directive that would have facilitated cross-border mergers by liberalizing and standardizing some of the regulations that apply to takeovers in each of the member countries. Even though some countries, such as Germany, disagree with some of the concepts in this reform, most of the EU countries agree and are likely to take action on their own, or have already done so.

In the US, numerous industries have witnessed unprecedented deregulation during the past five years, such as financial institutions and services, insurance, utilities, telecommunications, healthcare, and radio and television. Congress has enacted deregulatory legislation, such as the Telecommunications Act of 1996 and the partial repeal of the

Glass-Steagall Act in the Gramm-Leach-Bliley Act of 1999. In addition, the states have taken deregulatory action, such as permitting the demutualization of insurance companies. Much of this deregulatory activity has led to merger and acquisition activity.

Corporate community acceptance of hostile takeovers

In the US, hostile takeovers were viewed unfavorably during the 1980s as this technique was often used for the purpose of breaking up a company and selling its assets. Now, established companies have been willing to attempt hostile takeovers as part of a strategic plan to expand within an industry. These companies include General Electric, IBM, Johnson & Johnson, AT&T, Pfizer, and Wells Fargo. Another indication that hostile takeovers have become accepted is the acceptance by the corporate community of Delaware court decisions that support hostile bids, such as the decisions that banned dead-hand poison pills.

Pooling versus purchase accounting methodology

In the US, there has been a lot of controversy about the suitability of using the pooling method of accounting in mergers. The Financial Accounting Standards Board (FASB) has even gone so far as to propose eliminating its use entirely.[2] Accounting professionals have supported its elimination as a way to globally standardize merger accounting to the purchase method.[3] The seemingly inevitable demise of pooling accounting treatment for mergers in the US probably accelerated the pace of merger activity during the past two years.

The pooling and purchase methods differ dramatically, and it is no surprise that there is controversy over their use. Post-acquisition financial statements look enormously different depending on the method used, and the criteria for selection of the appropriate method are very technical. Generally, to use the pooling method, there must be a simple common stock for common stock exchange without any cash or other assets changing hands before or after the merger.[4] Minor technical deficiencies in the structuring of the merger transaction can mean that purchase accounting must be used.

In pooling, there is the assumption that the merger of the two entities is a mere amalgamation of two enterprises without either taking control of the other; the merged entity should be looked at as if it had been merged from inception. Pooling assumes that a fundamental change in the combined company has taken place at the time of the transaction. Thus, financial statements are recast to show the combined company as though it had always been one. In other words, historical balance sheet figures, income, expense and capital accounts are retroactively restated and asset values are shown at historical pre-transaction costs with partially depreciated values.

In purchase accounting, the transaction is viewed as though an asset was acquired (i.e. the second company). Because there is no fundamental change in the combined company, the historical accounts are not restated. Historical operations of the acquired entity are ignored for periods leading up to the purchase; operations (income and expenses) are added together for periods only after the transaction. Asset values are also treated differently. The historical value of the assets acquired in the merger is disregarded and new asset values for the acquired entity are assessed, based upon the valuation of those assets at – or shortly after – the merger.

In nearly every case, the combined company will look dramatically different depending on the method of accounting chosen. As a general rule, under pooling, both the historical and post-transaction income statements will show higher earnings – often significantly higher. This increase occurs because for the periods before the merger, historical earnings are added together; for periods after the merger, the depreciation and amortization levels for the assets are lower than they would have been if the assets were revalued as they are under purchase accounting.

Diminished antitrust concerns

Antitrust policy in any country can effectively prohibit mergers. Despite headline-grabbing announcements, antitrust enforcement is relatively limited today in all but the most extreme cases. US and EU antitrust regulators have been reasonably receptive to mergers because they appear to recognize that markets are global. With notable exceptions, a "big is bad" outlook by the regulators is not dominant and there appears to be little public fear of concentrated power (as reflected by the course of events in the Microsoft trial).

As a result, the size of the latest megamergers has been staggering. In cases in which the regulators have raised a red flag, they have accepted proposed divestitures and business restrictions to satisfy their concerns. However, there is growing evidence that the European Union may be somewhat more restrictive than the US at this time (e.g. the EU's position that scuttled the proposed General Electric-Honeywell merger). For more information about the impact of antitrust on technology companies, see Chapter 4.

Lower transactional taxes

The globalization of the markets makes it harder for countries to levy taxes on income from capital because the capital can move quite easily to another jurisdiction that has more favorable tax rates. In recognition of this, capital transaction taxes have declined steadily in most countries, particularly those where they had been quite high. This decline facilitates the ability of companies to conduct mergers since there is a reduced tax cost to doing a deal.

MARKET FACTORS

Market economics

Many economists believe that mergers and acquisitions activity helps the economy by causing assets to be moved to their best use. In addition, investors increasingly believe that the stock market tends to follow the level of mergers and acquisitions activity, or vice versa. In some respects, both of these contradictory notions are true. A hot stock market allows companies to use their equity as merger currency and gives them confidence to take bold steps to grow. On the other hand, during an active merger cycle, the level of takeover premiums built into stock prices tends to increase.

The ability of an acquiror to use equity or debt is critical to conduct a merger. If investors are willing to accept stock issued in mergers and encourage deals by supporting the stock of acquirors, companies will try to use stock if they view it as an overvalued acquisition currency. Similarly, if debt is also readily available at attractive rates, companies will use it to make acquisitions. For a number of years leading up to early 2000, the record high stock prices created many acquirors, particularly in the telecommunications, media, and technology industries. In addition, the bond market and bank loans were easy to tap. The falling stock market has dramatically impacted the availability of these sources of funds, and merger and acquisition activity has slowed considerably.

New technologies

Technological developments have led many established companies to remain competitive by acquiring smaller and more flexible companies. Seemingly impossible business combinations have become a reality. Mergers also enabled companies to spread the risk inherent in developing new technologies, particularly those engaged in significant research and development. For some companies, developing technology through mergers and acquisitions is viewed as necessary to survive in their rapidly changing industries. For more information about technology's impact on merger activity, see Chapter 4.

Industry consolidation

In the wake of consolidation in a number of deregulated industries, such as banking, telecommunications, and utilities, each company within those industries feels pressure to be a consolidator or begin contemplating who would be the best acquiror. Each time there is an acquisition in one of these industries, the remaining participants reassess their ability to continue as a stand-alone company. For other companies, there is a perceived need to quickly achieve economies of scale and diversify geographically. In some cases, an attempt to disrupt the announced merger by making a hostile bid is thought to be the last chance to remain independent.

Global competition

Many mergers are intended to achieve worldwide scale. As many of the largest product markets have become global in scope, the larger companies have sought to quickly penetrate local markets through acquisitions or joint ventures. Cross-border merger and acquisition activity has been increasing steadily and is expected to continue for many years. In particular, cross-border activity in Europe has skyrocketed on the heels of the creation of the euro. In addition, the Asian market has rebounded and the major thrust appears to be foreign investment into the Asian markets rather than the reverse as it had been for quite some time.

The growth of international transactions has created a greater need for – and has forced some – harmonization in the regulatory and accounting areas on a global scale. Further harmonization in the face of strong conflicting local interests continues to be the subject of debate. For more information on the global aspects of merger and acquisition activity, see Chapter 5.

Currency exchange rates

Currency fluctuations significantly impact the feasibility of cross-border mergers. The condition of the foreign exchange market dictates whether a particular cross-border merger becomes too expensive to effect or acts as an incentive to engage in such transactions. For example, European companies generally refrained from acquiring US companies when the value of the euro declined during 2000. On the other hand, the strong US dollar and weak Asian currencies led US companies to consider acquiring Asian companies. An acquiror should conduct a detailed analysis of the economy, trade deficit, and strength of the currency in the target's home country before entering into a cross-border transaction.

Novel merger and acquisition instruments and techniques

Perpetuated by the investment banking community, there is an endless string of innovative merger and acquisition techniques so that mergers and acquisitions can be accomplished in any possible circumstances. After new products are proven successful, companies often accept these innovative instruments. For example, the latest equity-based instruments include contingent value rights, tracking stock, and special kinds of preferred shares. Similarly, creativity in the junk bond and mezzanine funding markets is not unusual and can help fund an acquisition.

Bankers also have created numerous complex off-balance sheet financial structures to unlock liquidity from seemingly illiquid assets. For example, the musician David Bowie was able to securitize future earnings from his music so that he could reap the benefits of those earnings today. Companies can use these formerly illiquid assets as the assets necessary to engage in merger and acquisition activity.

Leveraged buyout funds

The size of LBO funds today is staggering and is a significant factor in fostering acquisition activity. These funds hold money solely for the purpose of engaging in leveraged buyouts. This money is partially responsible for the recent string of megadeals since much of this money is often underinvested and needs to find a "home."

Low inflation

Most debt pays interest at a nominal – rather than a real – rate. As a result, lower inflation means lower interest rates. In turn, acquirors pay higher prices for targets because they can get favorable acquisition financing. Inflation rates have generally been drifting lower in the developed world for several decades. Since many investors would react strongly to any country that dramatically raised borrowing rates, this trend is likely to continue.

The role of arbitrage

Arbitrageurs play a significant role in facilitating and promoting mergers. Together with hedge funds and activist institutional investors, they often encourage a company to seek a merger or to make an unsolicited bid for a company with which they are dissatisfied. By holding large amounts of a target's stock, they can help assure that the requisite shareholder vote is obtained.

MICRO-FACTORS

The number of possible micro-factors are too numerous to mention and unique to each particular transaction. However, there are several categories of micro-factors that typically play a role in a deal, although the type and extent of the role may vary.

Performance-related factors
Acquisition premiums

Acquisition premiums are critical to convincing a target's board to sell a company and to obtain the requisite target shareholder approval.

Average acquisition premiums vary depending on a number of variables, including expected growth rates in revenues, income and cash flow for the combined company, and the savings that a combination will produce. During the 1990s, based on the seller's closing price five business days before the initial announcement, average acquisition premiums varied from a low of 36% in 1997 to a high of 45% in 1995 and 44% in 1999. Interestingly, the average acquisition price earnings ratios did not increase at the same rate as the S&P 500 price earnings ratio and fell below the S&P 500 in 1998.[5]

Acquisition "currency"

Acquirors normally need ample cash or a high-flying stock price to engage in takeover activity. In deciding how to fund an acquisition, acquirors pay particular attention to how the acquisition will impact the acquiror's performance indicators, including the "multiples" within its industry (i.e. the numerator is the company's market capitalization and the denominator is the company's earnings). Before the bursting of the Internet bubble, there was a strong, high-multiple market in the technology, Internet and communications industries which allowed the more aggressive companies to go on an acquisition spree. During each merger wave, a source of "acquisition" currency propels the wave. During this wave, the record stock market made equity the primary source of acquisition currency. In the last wave, the fuel was junk bonds.

Creation of synergies

Many acquirors seek to buy targets with lower operating margins than themselves with the hope of creating synergies and saving costs. This normally is accomplished by spreading administrative overheads and eliminating redundant functions and personnel between the two companies, and ultimately improving the target's margins. In addition, acquirors may reallocate or redeploy the target's assets to more efficient uses. Many targets agree to merge in an effort to control costs and improve profit margin or eliminate overcapacity.

Shareholder activism

Over the past decade, shareholder activists have increasingly applied pressure on companies to restructure or seek a merger. In many cases, institutional investors cannot "exit" their investments due to the size of their holdings. As a result, institutional investors now recognize that they can increase the returns on their investments by actively monitoring corporate performance and communicating with the managers in their portfolio companies. If management does not adequately respond to their concerns, the investors often seek a change in control.

As many investors demand that the best practices of corporate governance flow from the US to other countries, this may be the "golden age" of corporate governance. In the US, shareholder activists have used shareholder proposals and other tactics to pressure companies to repeal classified boards, rescind poison pills, and reduce compensatory severance packages. The mere threat of soliciting proxies by activists has caused many companies to ease these types of acquisition roadblocks.

MANAGEMENT, EMPLOYEE AND CONSULTANT FACTORS

Sophisticated merger analysis

Companies can increasingly rely on experts that solely analyze and value mergers and acquisitions. These experts identify merger opportunities for their clients that might not otherwise be recognized. Some companies are in acquisition mode constantly and have these experts on their staff. Others rely on specialized investment banks, lawyers, consultants, and accountants to assist them in considering their strategic alternatives. The level of specialization can be quite narrow, such as experts in particular industries in particular countries.

Using improved technology, companies and their experts have better tools to evaluate potential combinations. Sophisticated modeling techniques enable them to review more accurate pro forma cash flows, earnings, and structuring scenarios. Sounder accounting regulations force companies to make more reliable financial data available to be used in these models. However, there still is a lack of accounting and disclosure standardization in the world as well as much unreliable or missing financial data.

Management severance arrangements

When approached with a takeover offer, the initial reaction of many managers is to resist since they do not wish to lose their job. For some time, boards of directors in the US have understood the need to provide incentive compensation, particularly stock options, to attract and retain talented management. This recognition extends to providing ample severance benefits to remove unnecessary management resistance to mergers. In fact, some shareholder activists believe that incentive severance packages in the US generally have grown too large.

In comparison, outside the US most countries have not embraced incentive compensation. However, there is a trend towards wider adoption of incentive compensation, including golden parachutes. For example, several years ago, Germany changed its rules to permit companies to grant stock options. As incentive compensation spreads, more mergers are likely to be accepted by entrenched management.

Management egos

Senior managers typically seek to grow their companies for two reasons. First, from an ego perspective, size matters when managers compare how their counterparts at other companies are faring. Second, growth often leads to higher compensation. As a result, managers normally are motivated to obtain greater market share – and mergers and acquisitions are the quickest way to reach this goal.

Employee and labor layoff concerns

Since mergers and acquisition often produce layoffs, employees generally do not like them. When the job market is vibrant, employee resistance to mergers is weaker, including the reaction by labor unions. Interestingly, many of the mergers during the past few years have been in industries with no – or weak – unions and hearty job opportunities, such as the technology and Internet industries.

In the US, record full employment during the past few years has led to heightened employee acceptance of mergers. Unemployment concerns have been greater in Europe, because unemployment rates are much higher than in the US and labor unions are stronger there. Strong European unions often successfully oppose takeovers in embattled industries but are not as aggressive in growing industries.

Concentrated management focus

As they first did when the "diversified conglomerate" concept failed in the late 1960s, companies again are recognizing that it is more efficient to focus on core businesses rather than attempt to operate myriad separate business units. It is not uncommon for larger companies to regularly sell or spin off non-core business units so that the business unit managers can properly focus on that unit's operations and so that the unit can achieve a higher valuation as a stand-alone entity. For more information about diversification strategies, see Chapter 3.

Acquisition exit strategies for new companies

Entrepreneurs increasingly build start-ups with the sole purpose of selling them. These entrepreneurs plan to be with a company only for a few years and hope that a more established company will buy them – before an initial public offering or after it. These normally are one-product technology companies that do not have the typical corporate infrastructure that would allow them to survive on their own for a long period.

As part of this exit strategy, a rapid time-to-market horizon for the product is critical since these companies will not be bought if their products are not up and running in the marketplace. Otherwise, the potential acquirors will fill the hole in their product line by either buying another start-up company or developing it themselves. For more information about how large technology companies make acquisitions, see Chapter 4.

LEARNING POINTS

The various macro- and micro-factors have differing impacts on merger activity.

Macro-factors:

» Deregulation
» Acceptance of hostile takeover techniques
» Pooling accounting treatment
» Antitrust concerns

» Transactional taxation
» Market economics
» New technologies
» Industry consolidation
» Global competition
» Currency exchange rates
» Novel techniques and instruments
» LBO funds
» Low inflation
» Arbitrage

Micro-factors:

» Levels of acquisition premiums
» Availability of acquisition currency
» Creation of synergies
» Shareholder activism
» Sophisticated merger analysis
» Management severance arrangements
» Management egos
» Employee layoff concerns
» Concentrated management focus
» Exit strategies for new companies

NOTES

1 Bruce Wasserstein, "*Big deal: the battle for control of America's leading corporations*," Warner Books, 1998.
2 Financial Accounting Standards Board Exposure Draft: Proposed Statement of Financial Accounting Standards, Business Combinations and Intangible Assets (Norwalk, Connecticut, September 1999).
3 *Ibid.* See also "Invitation to comment: methods of accounting for business combinations: recommendations of the G4 + 1 for achieving convergence"; Ollie S. Powers, "Accounting for

business combinations: a time for a change," *The National Public Accountant*, November 2000.

4 Accounting Principals Board Opinion #16, Paragraphs 46–48.

5 Joseph H. Flom, "Mergers & Acquisitions: The Decade in Review," 54 U. Miami L. Rev. 753, July 2000.

In Practice: M&A Success Stories

Chapter 7 details three recent public mergers and acquisitions, their negotiation terms, cultural, and governmental factors.

» the $183 billion merger between British telecom giant Vodafone Airtouch and German cellular provider Mannesmann;

» the $31 billion merger (some say acquisition) of the US auto maker Chrysler with the German auto maker Daimler-Benz; and

» the consolidation of three Japanese regional banks into the fourth largest bank in Japan, UFJ Bank, with over ¥1 trillion in capital.

Three mergers and acquisitions of public companies have been drawn from recent headlines to provide a comparison of how cultural and governmental factors influence the M&A decision-making process as well as a comparison of the process behind the hostile acquisition with a "friendly" merger. In the $183 billion hostile takeover of the German cellular provider Mannesmann by the British telecom giant Vodafone Airtouch, the process by which each management team used the media to support their own objectives is notable as well as how the threat of a proxy fight by an arbitrageur drove the final acquisition.

The merger of US auto maker Chrysler with German auto maker Daimler-Benz is indicative of the trend in cross-continental mergers, in this case of a European company merging with (some say acquiring) a US company. Topping the charts at that time at $31 billion, it was billed as the world's largest industrial merger. While Chrysler made every effort to ensure that this was a merger of equals, the German company clearly became the acquiror. Certain aspects of the German political environment (particularly the strength of the labor unions), as well as its evolving corporate law, determined whether the resulting company would be headquartered in the US or in Germany, or be multi-national, e.g. a Netherlands Antilles company.

The consolidation of three Japanese regional banks, Sanwa Bank, Tokai Bank and Toyo Trust, into the fourth largest bank in Japan created UFJ Bank, a mega-bank with over ¥1 trillion in capital. This three-way merger is indicative of how significantly the cultural and governmental attitudes once strongly against merger and acquisitions activity turned fully to encourage this financial consolidation.

VODAFONE-MANNESMANN MERGER

European companies contributed mightily to the international merger explosion that saw $3.2 trillion in deals during 2000. While much of the European merger and acquisition activity has been the result of friendly mergers, hostile takeovers are also becoming more prevalent. The $183 billion merger between Vodafone Airtouch and Mannesmann AG is not only indicative of the increased scale of European merger and acquisition activity but also shows the increased role hostile takeovers play in the global marketplace. Hostile takeovers had traditionally been frowned upon in most European nations, but new European Union rules have opened the door to this acquisition tactic. The Vodafone-Mannesmann merger is an example of how one company's threatened takeover can be an incentive to negotiate a merger.

The need to expand

The Vodafone-Mannesmann merger was driven by rapidly changing communications technology in Europe. Vodafone needed to increase its European presence if it hoped to compete in the global marketplace. It was already a major player in the 155 million-customer European cellular phone market when it first made overtures towards Mannesmann. European nations have a considerably higher percentage of cellular phone users than the United States, with over 55% of consumers in the EU being expected to use cellular technology by the end of 2001. Vodafone was the leading supplier of cellular products and services in Europe, a market share that stood to increase as the continent's population became increasingly reliant on cellular technology.

Vodafone sought this expansion opportunity because of emerging third-generation phone technology and increased competition from US providers. The company saw that third-generation phones would be capable of receiving high-speed data from the Internet and other online sources but would require major investments in infrastructure to create a network in Europe. Meanwhile, US providers began to catch up to their European counterparts in cellular technology and threatened to compete for European market share as their technology improved. Vodafone believed it needed to increase its market share in Europe if it was going to successfully build the infrastructure and take on media partners to establish a third-generation network. Consequently, Vodafone chairman Chris Gent began looking for merger opportunities early in 1998.

An unwilling suitor

While Vodafone was looking to acquire a partner to help it grow, Mannesmann had undergone its own round of expansion before its merger with Vodafone. Mannesmann spent $33 billion to acquire British cellular provider Orange in November 1999. That deal gave the German company a foothold in the British telecoms industry and established it as a serious competitor that Vodafone could not ignore.

Almost immediately after Mannesmann's acquisition of Orange, rumors started of a possible hostile takeover bid by Vodafone. On November 19, 1999, Chris Gent announced his company would offer Mannesmann shareholders €240 a share for their stock. Gent's announcement sounded alarms on both sides of the Atlantic due not only to the size of the proposed deal but also because there had never been a hostile takeover of this magnitude in Germany.

Mannesmann chairman Klaus Esser responded quickly to the offer, saying he did not want to merge regardless of the price offered. He then enlisted a team of advisors from Deutsche Bank, Merrill Lynch, and Morgan Stanley Dean Witter to help mount a defense of the company. Their strategy included selling off Mannesmann's automotive and engineering divisions, trying to acquire the French telecommunications company Vivendi, and appealing directly to shareholders in the European Union and the United States with large newspaper ads asking them to resist Vodafone's offer. These efforts were initially successful, as stock prices in both Vodafone and Mannesmann dropped during the week following the offer's announcement. One issue in particular that seemed to influence the stock market's reaction to the Vodafone bid was the estimated $36 billion in financing the company would need to close the deal. This would have been the largest corporate loan ever and signaled to many investors that Vodafone's takeover bid might have trouble getting off the ground.

Recapturing momentum

Chris Gent quickly rebounded from the offer's inauspicious start with his own media and speaking campaign to win over shareholders. He traveled to Germany to ensure workers that there would not be layoffs if Vodafone won the takeover battle and also pitched the long-term benefits that a merger would provide for both companies. Gent also moved quickly to preempt Mannesmann by agreeing to an Internet partnership with Vivendi, an offer that was more appealing to the French company than being bought outright by Mannesmann. These moves by Vodafone swung momentum towards the takeover bid and created unrest among Mannesmann shareholders.

Mannesmann was able to fight off a legal challenge by German shareholders that would have prevented the company from challenging the takeover bid, but then a larger problem developed. In December 1999, US arbitrageur Guy Wyser-Pratte, who had purchased a large chunk of Mannesmann stock in anticipation of a takeover, threatened a proxy fight to oust Mannesmann's management if it would not negotiate with Vodafone. Then in January 2000, four large institutional investors informed Esser that they planned to take Vodafone's offer. Faced with the prospect of losing a proxy fight and having new management determine the fortunes of his company, or losing outright in a hostile takeover, Esser sat down with Gent to work out a deal.

Saving face

Esser was not dealing from a position of strength, yet his work at the negotiating table drew praise from both industry analysts and shareholders. Most of the accolades were due to Esser's ability to drive up the price Vodafone paid for Mannesmann shares to €353 per share, a large increase for a stock that was only worth €263 when the takeover bid was launched. Mannesmann stockholders received 58.96 Vodafone shares for each Mannesmann share they held.

Esser was also credited for not erecting a "barbed wire" defense that would have taken advantage of Mannesmann bylaws that restricted any shareholder to only 5% of the votes. German law repealed this type of voting provision in the summer of 2000 because it severely restricted shareholder power, but Esser still could have relied on the bylaw in the final months prior to its repeal. The final agreement gave Mannesmann just over 49% of the new company and promised a healthy premium for the company's shareholders. The combination also ensured that with 42 million customers, Vodafone-Mannesmann would be the world's largest cellular provider, controlling 12% of the world cellular market, and would become the dominant player in European cellular service (Fig. 7.1).

While competitors in the European market hoped the European Commission would take a close look at the transaction, regulators quickly approved the union. Rival companies expressed concern about the size of the new company and the market share it would control, particularly with Mannesmann's acquisition of Orange within the year

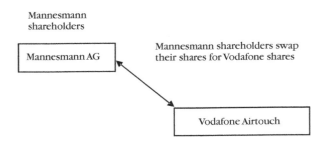

Fig. 7.1 The Vodafone-Mannesmann merger.

prior to the merger. Vodafone announced with the merger, however, that it planned to part with Orange, a divesture European regulators said was a must for the deal to be approved. The Commission's approval closed the world's largest transaction ever and further established that European companies would lead the way in the new wave of global mergers and acquisitions.

DAIMLER-CHRYSLER MERGER

The wave of European mergers in the past decade has drastically changed the way business is done on the continent. While European companies have traditionally avoided mergers and acquisitions, they are increasingly doing deals not only with fellow European companies but also spreading their reach across the Atlantic to the United States. The merger of German auto manufacturer Daimler-Benz and American carmaker Chrysler Corporation is indicative of this new trend in cross-continental mergers. The DaimlerChrysler union, however, is also a warning sign of the tremendous cultural and business challenges that confront companies attempting mergers in the global economy.

The DaimlerChrysler merger was billed as the world's largest industrial merger when it was announced in May 1998. The $31 billion deal combined two complementary suitors and promised to ensure each company's long-term viability. Chrysler, known for its ability to efficiently manufacture popular, cheap cars and light trucks, and Daimler-Benz, one of the world's leading manufacturers of luxury cars, hoped the combination of their different market shares and management styles would propel the new company into global competition. The companies' perceived strengths, however, have proven to be serious roadblocks to the merger's success. Both Chrysler and Daimler have encountered difficulty integrating the other's ideas into combined ventures and sagging profits at Chrysler have led to uneasiness among US shareholders. These problems have led some to question whether the union will last. While company executives dismiss suggestions of a breakup, a recent reorganization and proposed layoffs of Chrysler workers indicates that the merger has not progressed as the companies had hoped.

Complementary suitors

In the decade before the merger, Chrysler Corp. had grown to become the world's sixth largest auto manufacturer, largely due to its innovative models and manufacturing techniques. Chrysler introduced the minivan and the sport utility vehicle to the world and learned to compete with US auto behemoths GM and Ford by making these popular cars more efficiently than its competitors. The key to this efficiency was a dramatic alteration of purchasing agreements with Chrysler's parts suppliers. By forcing suppliers to assume as much as 70% of the manufacturing responsibilities for its cars, Chrysler drastically cut its production costs. This manufacturing innovation, combined with cutting-edge models such as the Viper and the Prowler, allowed Chrysler to become the US's hottest car manufacturer. Another key component to the company's success was its management team, headed by CEO Bob Eaton. Eaton created a management structure that was lean and allowed the company's design teams incredible flexibility to create new platforms. While Chrysler developed a reputation as the mavericks of the US auto industry under Eaton's direction, the company also saw record profits during the 1990s.

Chrysler's innovative, freewheeling reputation was in stark contrast to the staid culture of Daimler-Benz. Known primarily for its line of luxury cars and heavy trucks, the German manufacturing giant produced everything from planes to train engines in its 25 divisions. Under CEO Jurgen Schrempp, the company had grown to become the world's 15th largest auto maker, with its luxury models among the most sought-after in the world's developed nations. Schrempp guided Daimler-Benz through several reorganizations that cut its number of divisions from 35 to 25 and cost thousands of jobs. Schrempp, however, felt the company needed to open its mind to new design and management ideas, expand its production capacity, and increase its global market share to remain competitive. As a result, he sought out Eaton to discuss a possible union, and found a receptive audience.

Merger of equals

Bob Eaton feared that Chrysler was vulnerable in an economy that stressed global product exposure because it had not made inroads into the crucial European market, unlike competitors GM and Ford. That fear, as well as the opportunity to tap the technical and engineering resources of Daimler-Benz, convinced Eaton that the merger was crucial to Chrysler's survival. Schrempp sought Chrysler's innovation but, more importantly, needed an avenue into new markets such as Latin America, where Chrysler had an established presence. The result was a union announced on May 7, 1998 that the two CEOs billed as a merger of equals.

This billing was mainly an effort to save face for the US auto company whose pre-merger profits exceeded Daimler-Benz's. As Michigan State University economics professor Mordechai Kreini acknowledged, "this is likely to be more of a takeover than a merger." Under the deal's terms, Chrysler shareholders would hold 43% of the new company, with Daimler-Benz shareholders holding the remaining 57%. The deal was approved on September 18, 1998, with 97.5% of Chrysler shareholders and 99.9% of Daimler-Benz shareholders voting in favor. The merger was executed as a stock swap, with Chrysler shareholders receiving 0.6235 shares of DaimlerChrysler for each share they exchanged. Daimler-Benz shareholders engaged in a one-for-one share exchange.

Chrysler's primary goals were to maximize value and minimize taxes for its shareholders, and limit any post-merger opportunities for shareholders to challenge the deal. Daimler's objectives were a transaction that not only benefited its shareholders and was tax-free but also resulted in a German company. Its attorneys had argued for a straight merger with an exchange of Chrysler shares for Daimler shares. But Chrysler's attorneys would have none of it. A straight merger ran the horrific risk of an obscure German provision called a *spruchuerfahren*, which would allow any shareholder to challenge the stock valuation of the deal in a German court, even years after the merger was concluded. It was not practical to ask the US shareholders to vote for a straight merger where their stock values could be changed in the future.

An exchange offer, where the shareholders of Daimler and Chrysler would exchange their shares for shares of a new company, avoided the dreaded *spruchuerfahren*. It had another benefit as well. An exchange would allow the merged company to petition the US Securities and Exchange Commission for an accounting advantage called a "pooling of interests." Under SEC rules, if 90% of shareholders of both companies exchanged their stock for newly created shares in a merged entity, then Daimler and Chrysler could pool their interests. The pooling move, though strictly a bookkeeping maneuver, was important. Without pooling, the merged company's earnings would be artificially depressed by an estimated $925 million per year.

As to the nationality of the surviving entity, a German company, an "AG" (*Aktiengesellschaft*), would allow for a tax-free exchange, as well as the only viable solution politically for the German company. Under German law, companies were governed by "codetermination" in which half of the members of the supervisory board were elected officials of the labor force. Codetermination was an absolute tenet of German democracy. For the Germans, to allow the company founded by the inventor of the automobile to go outside Germany was unacceptable. The sticky point of the name was also left until the final moments before the boards voted on the deal. Eaton wanted "Chrysler Daimler-Benz" but finally accepted "DaimlerChrysler" after Daimler dropped "Benz" and agreed to a board-related concession. In the same way as the nationality of the surviving company, the German people would never accept the Daimler name to be perceived as subordinate (Fig. 7.2).

Officials from the newly formed company immediately talked of the expected $3 billion in savings that DaimlerChrysler would realize in its first five years by sharing research and development, purchasing, and components. There were optimistic forecasts of joint manufacturing initiatives and design teams. DaimlerChrysler sailed through reviews by antitrust regulators in both the US and the European Union as the companies had no major overlapping products or markets. Reaction

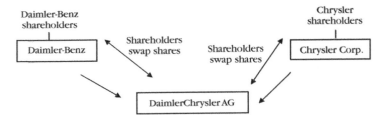

Fig. 7.2 The DaimlerChrysler merger.

on Wall Street was also positive as Chrysler stock jumped $7.38 after the announcement to finish at $48.81 while Daimler's shares were up $6.50 to finish at $108.56. Daimler-Benz chairmen Schrempp predicted success for the merger because "the two companies are a perfect fit of two leaders in their respective markets." This post-deal enthusiasm would soon be tempered by the harsh realities of melding two foreign corporations of vastly different business cultures.

Clash of cultures

Among the first illusions to be cast aside following the deal's consummation was the concept of a merger of equals. Daimler-Benz had purchased Chrysler, despite the US corporation's larger profits, and its leaders and culture would rule the new venture. This control issue became clear to Chrysler managers during initial planning meetings with their German counterparts and set a contentious tone for many of their early encounters. While both companies hoped to draw on the different management and creative strengths of the other, the two parties also found it difficult to understand the other's way of thinking. US managers chafed at the Germans' penchant for long-term planning, while the Germans could not fathom the Americans' willingness to part with plans laid out precisely and move in new directions. Design technicians from both sides also noticed reluctance by their new counterparts to share technology and ideas. Efforts to figure out a balance between the two cultures were not helped when Bob Eaton announced in May 1998 that he would step down as co-chairman within three years of signing the deal. To many of the players on both sides of the Atlantic, Eaton's planned exit signaled a capitulation by Eaton and Chrysler and further confirmed DaimlerChrysler's status as a German company.

In addition to cultural differences, DaimlerChrysler has also struggled with shrinking profits in the Chrysler division, where profits dropped from €5.2 billion in 1998 to €500 million in 2000, with continuing profit declines, and even losses, expected into 2002. This downturn has been blamed on several factors, including DaimlerChrysler being rejected by the S&P 500 due to its heavy foreign investment base, an exodus of talented Chrysler managers, and a shrinking US economy. DaimlerChrysler's response has been a massive reorganization that promises to cut the number of models offered by Chrysler while also closing six production plants and eliminating 26,000 jobs.

An incomplete picture

While media reports and financial returns indicate the DaimlerChrysler deal is faltering, company executives point to several initiatives that show how the two entities are growing together. In 1999 the company began producing Jeep Cherokees on the same Austrian production line as Mercedes vehicles. DaimlerChrysler has also seen drastic savings by producing parts in US factories and then shipping them back to Germany for assembly. These steps, as well as the Chrysler reorganization, indicate that the new company may be turning the corner and the merger shaking off its reputation of a failed venture. Despite these positive signs, however, DaimlerChrysler is still widely viewed as an example of the potential stumbling blocks in a transatlantic merger.

THREE-WAY MERGER/CONSOLIDATION INTO UFJ GROUP

Merger and acquisition activities have been historically rare in Asia, and rarer still in Japan. Hostile acquisitions almost never occur, though there were three unsolicited tender offers in Japanese firms by foreign firms in 2000 and 2001. Mergers are generally discouraged due to a number of factors among public companies in Japan. Cross-ownership among industry giants is common through phalanxes of "stable shareholders," composed of major banks, suppliers, and *keiretsu* members. These shareholders are still not primarily motivated to sell by stock price. A 2001 publication noted that of the top 25 firms with high break-up values in relation to market capitalization, 23 had "stable shareholders" representing over 50% of total shares owned. Hostile deals are unlikely, though friendly acquisitions and mergers are on the rise. Another factor encouraging the increase of merger and acquisition is the long-drawn-out recession in Japan. This has softened the government as well as industry view that combinations may create stability and dampen the "Japan Inc." engine.

There are several key differences in the (generally) similar legal framework between the US and Japan regarding mergers and acquisitions. The most important is that due to the inadequacy of public company disclosure, greater due diligence is necessary in Japan. The timeline is, as a result, greatly extended. This is true for foreign acquirors as well as domestic acquirors, though to the extent that there is common ownership within an industry, an undue advantage is held by Japanese acquirors of other firms. This is the case in heavy industry, particularly automotive, but also in the financial sector. In the past several years, substantial merger activity has resulted in consolidations in the banking sector of the Japanese economy. One notable example is the consolidation of three national banks into one mega-bank, UFJ Bank, creating the fourth largest financial institution in Japan, and one of the largest able to compete on a global stage.

UFJ was formed by the consolidation of three large regional Japanese banks, the Sanwa Bank, the Tokai Bank, and the Toyo Trust and Banking Co. Sanwa's president, Kaneo Muromachi, was seen as the driving force and became the chairman of the UFJ board. He had approached the head of Tokai, Hideo Ogasowara, as both were the leading financial institutions in their own regions, Tokyo and Nagaya respectively. The financial sector readily recognized that their business units, particularly retail and corporate banking, could be easily consolidated. As regional banks, their geographic "footprints" complemented each other perfectly and while some overlap exists, savings through closing redundant branches were clearly identifiable.

As with other mergers, regional feelings played a role, so much so that the location of the headquarters was not agreed upon until days before the merger announcement. Other decisions were also delayed to allow for the procedure to continue smoothly. Some items that to an outsider would seem to be the most critical, such as the exchange values given to each company's shares, were delayed so that a merger of equals could be touted to the respective shareholders.

Shunroku Yokoshuka, president of Toyo, reportedly won over Muromachi and Ogasowara (and eventually all the banks' shareholders) with the notion that rather than try to merge into the largest retail and commercial bank possible, they should strive to provide more comprehensive banking services to their clientele – not only retail and commercial banking but also trust services, securities and asset management, and investment banking. Providing more depth to the services on offer was to be the deciding factor in assuring client loyalty and the firm's success and stability in the global banking marketplace.

This consolidation was also unique in that the three heads looked to create an organization that could enhance corporate growth and shareholder value through the establishment of a system of corporate governance that allowed for speedy and transparent management. To create a streamlined system, Muromachi, Yokoshuka, and Ogasowara determined that there should be a balance of power between the board and the executive officers. The roles of the "president" and the "chairman" would be clearly separated. Further, over half of the board would consist of non-executive directors, including several outside directors (extremely unusual in a Japanese public company). The board would have 12 directors, an unheard of number, most being two to three times the size, aiming to facilitate quicker and more responsive decision making. Further, the various committees, such as compliance and compensation committees, would be comprised mainly of outside directors.

The financial markets reacted positively to the merger announcement. The positive effects were recognized as including cost reductions, expansion of earning opportunities, targeting of attainable goals, and additional synergies. Cost reductions would occur through restructuring and revitalizing all layers of management, including overlapping operations among the domestic and overseas branch networks and the head offices. Over the first three years, 58 domestic branches and 19 overseas branches would be closed, eliminating 4400 positions (a further consolidation of 68 domestic and 13 overseas branches, representing 3100 employees, was planned through 2006). Further, significant savings would be achieved by introducing a more advanced information technology infrastructure. These IT-related savings were projected at almost ¥50 billon through cutting positions and combined purchasing. Though the overall costs of integrating the three banks was estimated to exceed ¥150 billion by 2006, the net integration effect would be over ¥100 billion in the block with ¥88 billion in increased synergies and ¥175 billion in rationalizations.

The merger was recognized as allowing significant expansion of earning opportunities through providing innovative and comprehensive financial services throughout the expanded and combined new market areas. In particular, as a result of the participation of Toyo, functions to be provided to corporate customers would be significantly enhanced in areas such as corporate agency, pension trust, and real estate-related services. In the retail market businesses, Toyo would strengthen asset management, testamentary trust, and real estate businesses. By consolidating their operations into one of the four largest financial firms, Sanwa, Toyo, and Tokai could more easily target and attain financial goals. Net profits, for example, were estimated to rise from ¥850 billion (unconsolidated) to ¥1000 billion (consolidated) by 2006. By business unit, retail banking would grow from ¥79 billion to almost ¥300 billion by 2006, corporate banking would grow from ¥375 billion to ¥550 billion by 2006, global banking would grow from ¥90 billion to ¥150 billion by 2006, trust services would grow from ¥25 billion to ¥55 billion by 2006, asset management would grown from ¥7 billion to 17 billion by 2006, and securities/investment banking would increase from ¥26 billion to ¥60 billion by 2006. Consolidated net business profit was estimated to grow from more than ¥700 billion to over ¥1000 billion by 2006.

Glossary

Chapter 8 includes an A–Z glossary of mergers and acquisitions.

Acquisition – The purchase of an entire company or a controlling interest in a company.

Antigreenmail amendment – A corporate charter amendment that prohibits targeted share purchases at a premium from an outside shareholder without the approval of non-participating shareholders.

Antitakeover amendment – A corporate charter amendment that is intended to make takeovers more difficult and/or expensive for an unwanted bidder.

Any-or-all tender offer – A tender offer for an unspecified number of shares in a target company.

Appraisal rights – The rights of shareholders to obtain an independent valuation of their shares to determine the appropriate value. Shareholders may pursue these rights in litigation.

Back-end rights plan – A type of poison pill antitakeover defense whereby shareholders are issued a rights dividend that is exercisable in the event that a hostile bidder purchases a certain number of shares. Upon the occurrence of that event, shareholders may then exchange their rights combined with their shares for a certain amount of cash and/or other securities equal to a value that is set by the target. In doing so, the target's board, in effect, establishes a minimum price for the company's stock.

Bear hug – An offer made directly to the board of directors of a target company. Usually made to increase the pressure on the target with the threat that a tender offer may follow.

Bidder – The acquiring firm.

Blended price – The weighted average price that is set in a two-tiered tender offer.

Board out clause – An antitakeover provision that allows the board of directors to decide when a supermajority provision is effective.

Breakup fees – The payments that the target gives the bidder if the target decides to cancel the transaction.

Business judgment rule – The legal principle that assumes the board of directors is acting in the best interests of shareholders unless it can be clearly established that it is not. If that is established, the board would be in violation of its fiduciary duty to shareholders.

Bustup takeover – A takeover in which an acquisition is followed by the sale of certain, or even all, of the assets of the target company. This is sometimes done to pay down the debt used to finance a leveraged acquisition.

Classified board – Also called a **staggered board**. An antitakeover measure that separates the firm's board of directors into different classes with different voting rights. The goal is to make acquisition of voting rights more difficult.

Coercive tender offer – A tender offer that exerts pressure on target shareholders to tender early. This pressure may come in the form of preferential compensation for early tendering shareholders. Changes in securities laws have limited the effectiveness of such tender offers.

Collar agreement – Agreed-upon adjustments in the number of shares offered in stock-for-stock exchange to account for fluctuations in stock prices before the completion of the deal.

Corporation – The most common form of business organization, in which the total worth of the organization is divided into shares of stock, each share representing a unit of ownership. A corporation is characterized by a continuous life span and the limited liability of its owners.

Cramdown – A situation that occurs when a reorganization plan is approved even when some classes of creditors do not approve it. At least one class of creditors needs to approve the plan for there to be a cramdown.

Cumulative voting rights – When shareholders have the right to pool their votes to concentrate them on the election of one or more directors rather than apply their votes to the election of all directors.

Dead hand provisions – Antitakeover measure that gives the power to redeem a poison pill to the directors who were on the target's board of directors before the takeover attempt.

Due diligence – (a) The reasonable investigation performed by the underwriter and mandated by the SEC to protect the investing public who may fairly rely on an underwriter's conduct. (b) The reasonable investigation performed by the acquiror prior to the purchase of a business.

Economies of scope – The ability of a firm to utilize one set of inputs to provide a broader range of outputs or services.

Exclusivity period – The time period following a Chapter 11 filing when only the debtor can put forward a reorganization plan. It is initially 120 days, but the time period is often extended.

Fair price provision – An antitakeover charter amendment that requires the payment of a certain minimum price for the shares of the target. It increases the bidder's cost of a takeover and makes coercive actions, such as two-tiered tender offers, less effective.

Flip-in poison pill plan – The most commonly used poison pill antitakeover defense, in which shareholders are issued rights to purchase common stock in a bidding firm's company at a significant discount, usually 50%.

Front end-loaded tender offers – A tender offer in which the compensation of a first tier is superior to a later second tier. Such offers are designed to be coercive and cause shareholders to tender early.

Going private – When a public corporation becomes privately held. This is usually done through a leveraged buyout.

Golden parachute – Employment contract of upper management that provides a larger payout upon the occurrence of certain control transactions, such as a certain percentage share purchase by an outside entity or when there is a tender offer for a certain percentage of the company's shares.

Greenmail – The payment of a premium above current market price for the shares held by a certain shareholder, with the goal of eliminating that shareholder as a threat to the company's independence.

Hart-Scott-Rodino Antitrust Improvements Act of 1976 – A law that requires a bidding company to file with the US Federal Trade Commission and the US Justice Department and receive antitrust approval from one of these entities before completing a takeover.

Herfindahl-Hirschman (HH) Index – The sum of the squares of the market shares of companies in a given industry. It is a measure of industry concentration and is more sensitive to the effects of mergers than simple market shares.

Highly confident letter – A letter issued by an investment bank indicating that it is confident that it can raise the necessary financing for a takeover.

Holding company – A company that owns the stock of other corporations. A holding company may not engage in actual operations of its own but merely manages various operating units in which it owns an interest.

In play – When the market believes that a company may be taken over. At this time, the stock becomes concentrated in the hands of arbitrageurs and the company becomes vulnerable to a takeover and the target of a bid.

Inside information – Material information that has not been disseminated to, or is not readily available to, the general public.

Insider – Any person who has or has access to material nonpublic information about a corporation. Insiders include directors, officers, and stockholders who own more than 10% of any class of equity security of a corporation.

Joint venture – When companies jointly pursue a certain business activity.

Junk bond – High-yield bonds that receive a rating from Standard & Poor's (or other agency) of BB or below. Such bonds are riskier than investment-grade bonds, which have higher ratings.

LBO – See **Leveraged buyout.**

LBO funds – A pool of investment capital that invests in various leveraged buyouts seeking to realize the high returns potentially available in LBOs while lowering risk through diversification.

LOI – Letter of intent. (a) The agreement signed by a company and its underwriter to document its understanding of expected offering price, underwriter's discount and the responsibility for expenses while pursuing the IPO. (b) The agreement signed by a company and an acquiror to document their understanding of expected purchase price, purchase terms, time line, and what is expected of the parties prior to drafting a definitive purchase and sale agreement.

Leveraged buyout (LBO) – The purchase of a company that is financed primarily by debt. However, the term is more often applied to debt-financed going-private transactions.

Lockup option – An option to buy certain valuable assets or stock in the target, which it issues to a friendly party. If the option limits the bidding process, it could be challenged legally.

Management buyout (MBO) – A going-private transaction in which the management of a company or division of a company takes the company or division private.

Merger – Combining two or more companies by offering the stockholders of one company securities in another company in exchange for the surrender of their stock.

No-shop provisions – Where a seller agrees not to solicit or enter into sale agreements with any other bidders.

Note purchase rights – Another name for back-end poison pill plans.

Option – A security that represents the right to buy or sell a specified amount of an underlying security at a specified price within a specified time. The purchaser acquires a right, and the seller assumes an obligation.

Pac-Man defense – One of the more extreme antitakeover defenses. It refers to a situation in which a target makes a counteroffer for the bidder.

Partial tender off – A tender offer for less than all of a target's outstanding shares.

PIK debt securities – Bonds that may pay bondholders compensation in a form other than cash.

Poison pill – A right issued by a corporation as a preventative antitakeover defense. It allows right holders to purchase shares in either their own company or the combined target and bidder companies at a discount, usually 50%. This discount may make the takeover prohibitively expensive.

Poison put – A provision added to bond indenture contracts that allows bondholders to sell or ''put'' their bonds back to the issuing corporation at a predetermined exercise price. Poison puts became popular in the leveraged buyout era of the 1980s, when bond prices plummeted in response to the increased debt loads of post-LBO companies and the subsequent downgrading of the debt.

Preferred stock plans – Early version of poison pills that used preferred stock as opposed to rights.

Proxy – A limited power of attorney from a stockholder authorizing another person to vote on stockholder issues according to the first stockholder's instructions. In order to vote on corporate matters, a stockholder must either attend the annual meeting or must vote by proxy.

Proxy contest – When a dissident shareholder or group of shareholders try to take control of the board of directors or use the process to enact certain changes in the activities of the company.

Pure plays – Companies that operate within clearly defined market boundaries.

Put – An option contract giving the owner the right to sell a specified amount of an underlying security at a specified price within a specified time.

Recapitalization plan – The alteration of the capital structure of a company that adds debt and may reduce equity. It often is used as an antitakeover device when a target uses it as an alternative offer to a hostile bid. It often involves assuming considerable debt and paying a superdividend to target shareholders.

Reverse LBO – Companies that go public after having gone private in a leveraged buyout.

Reverse split – A reduction in the number of a corporation's shares outstanding that increases the par value of its stock or its earnings per share. The market value of the total number of shares remains the same.

Revlon duties – Legal principle that actions, such as antitakeover measures, that promote a value-maximizing auction process are allowable whereas those that thwart it are not.

Roll-up acquisitions – An acquisition program that features multiple acquisitions of smaller companies by a larger consolidator.

Schedule 13D or 13G – The document that is required by the Williams Act to be filed with the SEC within 10 days of acquiring 5% or more of a public company's outstanding shares. This filing discloses certain information, including the purchaser's identity and intentions, as well as other related information, such as financing sources, in the case of a planned takeover.

Schedule 14D – The document that, pursuant to the Williams Act, must be filed with the SEC by the initiator of a tender offer. This filing discloses information on the identity of the bidder, specifics of the offer, and other relevant information, such as sources of financing and post-acquisition plans.

Scorched-earth defense – An antitakeover defense that has such an adverse effect on the target that it renders it undesirable to bidders.

Sell-off – A general term describing a sale of a part of a company. It also includes other more specific transactions, such as divestitures or spin-offs.

Shark repellent – Another name for an antitakeover defense.

Spin-off – A type of sell-off in which a parent company distributes shares on a pro rata basis to its shareholders. These new shares give shareholders ownership rights in a division or part of the parent company that is sold off.

Split-off – A type of sell-off in which shareholders of a parent company exchange their shares in the parent company for shares in the sold-off entity.

Split-up – When the parent company spins off all of its component parts and ceases to exist.

Standstill agreement – An agreement that a potential hostile bidder enters into with the target corporation whereby the bidder agrees, in exchange for some consideration, not to purchase more than an agreed-upon number of shares.

Strategic alliance – A more flexible alternative to a joint venture whereby certain companies agree to pursue certain common activities and interests.

Stock parking – The attempt to evade the disclosure requirements of securities law by keeping shares in names other than that of the true owner.

Street sweeps – Open-market purchases of a target's stock that are not tender offers and therefore are not subject to the requirements of the Williams Act.

Supermajority provision – A preventative antitakeover defense that amends the corporate charter to require a higher majority, such as two-thirds or even more, to approve certain transactions such as mergers.

Targeted share repurchase – Refers to repurchase of stock of a large shareholder, such as a hostile bidder. It usually is done at a premium over market prices. This type of transaction is also referred to as **greenmail**.

Tax-free reorganizations – Types of business combinations in which shareholders do not incur tax liabilities. There are four types – A, B, C, and D – which differ in various ways, including the amount for stock and/or cash that is offered.

Tender offer – An offer made directly to shareholders. One of the more common ways hostile takeovers are implemented.

Tombstone ad – An advertisement for the sale of a security that is placed by investment bankers to call attention to their prospectus. Also describes a post-sale or post-funding announcement of a deal that has been completed that may be published to announce the contribution of an advisor or the participation of an investor in the deal.

Two-tiered tender offer – Tender offers in which the bidder offers a superior first-tier price for a maximum number of shares while it offers to acquire the remaining shares in the second tier at a lower price.

Unocal standard – The legal principle that reasonable defensive measures that are consistent with the business judgment rule are legally acceptable.

Voting plans – A variation on the poison pill defense theme. They allow preferred stockholders to have supervoting rights if a bidder acquires a certain percentage of the target's stock. They are designed to prevent a bidder from getting voting control of the target.

White knight – A more acceptable buyer that a target of a hostile bid may approach.

White squire – A friendly company or investor that purchases an interest in the target of a hostile bid. The target may do this to make a takeover more difficult.

Resources

Chapter 9 provides a brief summary listing, including:

» seminal books;
» useful publications and Websites;
» international treaties; and
» associations.

BOOKS

Addo, Charles, *Corporate Mergers and Acquisitions: a case study*, iUniverse, Incorporated, 2000.

Anders, George, *Merchants of Debt; KKR and the Mortgaging of American Business*, Basic Books, 1992.

Auletta, Ken, *Greed and Glory on Wall Street: the fall of the House of Lehman*, Warner Brooks, 1987.

Auletta, Ken, *The Highwaymen: warriors of the Information Superhighway*, Random House, 1997.

Baird, Douglas, "The uneasy case for corporate reorganizations," 15, *Journal of Legal Studies* 127, 1986.

Bauman, Robert P., *From Promise to Performance: a journey of transformation at Smithkline Beecham*, Harvard Business School Publishing, 1997.

Bebchuk, Lucian, "A new approach to corporate reorganizations," 101 Harv. L. Rev. 775, 1986.

Bendaniel, David J. & Rosenbloom, Arthur, *International M&A, Joint Ventures and Beyond: doing the deal*, John Wiley & Sons, 1997.

Blum, Walter & Katz, Wilbur, "Depreciation and enterprise valuation," 32 U. Chi. L. Rev. 236, 1965.

Blum, Walter, "The law and language of corporate reorganization," 17 U. Chi. L. Rev. 565, 1950.

Bollenbacher, George M., *The New Business of Banking: transforming challenges into opportunities in today's financial services marketplace*, Irwin Professional Publications, 1995.

Borghese, Robert J. & Morin, Paul, *M&A from Planning to Integration*, McGraw-Hill Education Group, 2001.

Brealey, Richard & Myers, Stewart, *Principals of Corporate Finance*, 6th edn, 2000.

Brooks, John, *The Go-Go Years*, Dutton, 1984.

Brooks, John, *The Takeover Game*, Truman Talley Books/Dutton, 1987.

Bruck, Connie, *The Predators' Ball. The inside story of Drexel Burnham and the rise of the junk bond raiders*, Penguin USA, 1989.

Bryer, Lanning G., *Mergers and Acquisitions in Intellectual Property*, John Wiley & Sons, 2001.

Caplan, Lincoln, *Skadden: Power, Money and the Rise of a Legal Empire*, Farrar Straus & Giroux, 1994.

Chandler, Alfred D. & Daems, Herman, *Managerial Hierarchies: comparative perspectives on the rise of the modern industrial enterprise*, Harvard University Press, 1980.

Chernow, Ron, "House of Morgan," *Atlantic Monthly Press*, 1990.

Clemente, Mark N. & Greenspan, David S., *Winning at Mergers and Acquisitions: the guide to market focused planning and integration*, John Wiley & Sons, 1998.

Clurman, Richard M., *To the End of Time: the seduction and conquest of a media empire*, Simon & Schuster, 1992.

Cohen, Herb, *You Can Negotiate Anything*, Bantam, 1989.

Coll, Steve, *The Deal of the Century: the breakup of AT&T*, Atheneum, 1986.

Colomiris, Charles, "Is the bank merger wave of the 1990s efficient? Lessons from nine case studies, studies on financial market deregulation," American Enterprise Institute for Public Policy Research, 1998.

Copeland, Tom, Kollet, Tim & Murin, Jack, *Valuation: measuring and managing the value of companies*, John Wiley & Sons, 1995.

Cottle, Sidney, Murray, Roger F. & Block, Frank E., *Graham and Dodd's Security Analysis*, McGraw-Hill, 1988.

Cray, Ed, *Chrome Colossus: General Motors and its times*, McGraw-Hill, 1980.

Dunlap, Albert Jr. & Andelman, Bob, *Mean Business: how I save bad companies and make good companies great*, Simon & Schuster, 1997.

Dymski, Gary A., "The Bank Merger Wave: the economic causes and social consequences of financial consolidation," *Issues in Money, Banking and Finance*, Sharpe, M.e., Inc., 2001.

Evans, Frank C. & Bishop, David M., *Valuation for M&A: building value in private companies*, John Wiley & Sons, 2001.

Feldman, Mark L. & Spratt, Michael Frederick, *Five Frogs on a Log: a CEO's field guide to accelerating the transition in mergers, acquisitions and gut wrenching change*, HarperCollins, 1998.

Ferrera, Ralph C., Brown, Meredith M. & Hall, John H., *Takeover: attack and survival, a strategist's manual*, Michie Dullerworth, 1987.

Fischel, Daniel, *Payback: the conspiracy to destroy Michael Milken and his financial revolution*, HarperBusiness, 1996.

Fisher, Roger and Ury, William, *Getting to Yes: how to negotiate agreement without giving in*, Simon & Schuster, 1987.

Fleischer, Jr, Arthur & Sussman, Alexander R., *Takeover Defense*, Aspen Law & Business, 1995.

Flowers, Edward B., *US Utility Mergers and the Restructuring of the New Global Power Industry*, Greenwood Publishing Group, Incorporated, 1998.

Freund, James C., *Anatomy of a Merger: strategies and techniques for negotiating corporate acquisitions*, Law Journal Seminars Press, 1975.

Galbraith, John, *The Great Crash – 1929*, Houghton Mifflin, 1988.

Gaughan, Patrick A., *Merger, Acquisitions, and Corporate Restructurings*, John Wiley & Sons, 1996.

Groner, Alex, *The American Heritage History of American Business and Industry*, American Heritage, 1972.

Grover, Ron, *The Disney Touch: how a daring management team revived an entertainment empire*, Irwin Professional Publications, 1996.

Gupta, Udayan, *Done Deals: venture capitalists tell their stories*, Harvard Business School Publishing, 2000.

Hamel, Gary & Prahalad, C.K., *Competing for the Future*, Harvard Business School Press, 1994.

Harvard Business Review on Mergers & Acquisitions, 2001.

Harvey, Thomas W., *The Banking Revolution: positioning your bank in the new financial services marketplace*, Irwin Professional Publications, 1996.

Hesson, Robert, *Steel Titan: the life of Charles M. Schwab*, University of Pittsburgh Press, 1990.

Jacobs, Michael T., *Short-Term America: the causes and cures of our business myopia*, Harvard Business School Press, 1991.

Johnston, Moira, *Takeover: the new Wall Street warriors: the men, the money, the impact*, Arbor House, 1986.

Kelly, Edmund J. & Pryor, Tim, *The Takeover Dialogues: a discussion of hostile takeovers*, iUniverse, Incorporated, 2001.

Lacey, Robert, *Ford: the men and the machine*, Little, Brown, 1986.

Lajoux, Alexandra Reed & Elson, Charles M., *The Art of M&A Due Diligence*, McGraw-Hill, 2000.

Lajoux, Alexandra Reed *et al.*, *Art of M&A: financing and refinancing*, McGraw-Hill, 1999.

Lindskoog, Nils, *Long Term Greedy: the triumph of Goldman Sachs*, McCrossen Publishing, 1999.

Linenkugel, Nancy. *Lessons from Mergers: Voices of Experience*. Health Administration, 2000.

MacDonald, Larry, *Nortel Networks: how innovation and vision created a network giant*, John Wiley & Sons, 2000.

Madigan, Charles & Martinez, Arthur C., *Hard Road to the Softer Side: lessons from the transformation of Sears*, Crown Publishing Group, 2001.

Mair, George, *The Barry Diller Story: the life and times of America's greatest entertainment mogul*, John Wiley & Sons, 1997.

Mark, Howard, *Financial Shenanigans: how to detect accounting gimmicks and fraud in financial reports*, McGraw-Hill, 1993.

Mayer, Martin, *The Bankers. The Next Generation*, Dutton, 1997.

McCauley, Robert N., *Dodging Bullets: changing US corporate capital structure in the 1980s and 1990s*, MIT Press, 1999.

McKee, Carl W., *Japanese Takeovers*, Harvard Business School Press, 1991.

McKibben, Gordon, *Cutting Edge: Gillette's journey to global leadership*, Harvard Business School Publishing, 1997.

Silver, A. David., *Middle-Market Business Acquisition Directory and Source Book*, HarperInformation, 1990.

O'Glove, Thornton L., with Robert Sobel, *Quality of Earnings: the investor's guide to how much money a company is really making*, The Free Press, 1987.

Paulson, Ed, *Inside Cisco: the real story of sustained M&A growth*, John Wiley & Sons, 2001.

Petzinger, Thomas & Petzinger, Jr, Thomas, *Oil & Honor: the Texaco-Pennzoil wars*, Beard Books, Incorporated, 1999.

Pickens, T. Boone, *Boone*, Random House, 1988.

Porter, Michael E., *Competitive Strategy: techniques for analyzing industries and competitors*, The Free Press, 1984.

Ramu, S. Shiva, *Corporate Growth Through Mergers and Acquisitions*, Sage Publications, 1998.

Reed, Stanley F., *The M&A Deskbook*, McGraw-Hill, 1998.

Reich, Cary, *Financier: the biography of Andre Meyer: a story of money, power and the reshaping of American business*, William Morrow, 1983.

Rezaee, Zabihollah, *Financial Institutions, Valuations, Mergers and Acquisitions*, John Wiley & Sons, 2001.

Rogers, David, *The Future of American Banking: managing for change*, McGraw-Hill, 1992.

Salsbury, Stephen, *No Way to Run a Railroad: the untold story of the Penn Central crisis*, McGraw-Hill, 1982.

Sirower,Mark L., *The Synergy Trap: how companies lose the acquisition game*, Simon & Schuster Trade, 1997.

Slater, Robert, *The New GE: how Jack Welch revived an American institution*, Irwin Professional Publications, 1992.

Sloan, Alfred P., *My Years with General Motors*, Doubleday, 1996.

Smith, Roy C., *The Money Wars*, Truman Talley Books, 1990.

Sobel, Robert, *Dangerous Dreamers: the financial innovators from Charles Merrill to Michael Milken*, John Wiley & Sons, 1993.

Spiegal, John, Gart, Alan & Gart, Steven, *Banking Redefined: how superregional powerhouses are reshaping financial services*, Irwin Professional Publications, 1996.

Steiner, Peter O., *Mergers, Motives, Effects, Policies*, University of Michigan Press, 1975.

Stevens, Mark, *King Icahn: the biography of a renegade capitalist*, Dutton, 1993.

Stewart, James B., *Den of Thieves*, Touchstone, 1992.

Stone, Dan G., *April Fools: an insider's account of the rise and collapse of Drexel Burnham*, Donald I. Fine, 1990.

Tarbell, Ida, *History of the Standard Oil Company*, Amereon Ltd, 1993.

Thornhill, William T., *Forensic Accounting. How to Investigate Financial Fraud*, Irwin Professional Publications, 1994.

Tom, Willard K. & Lipsky, Jr, Abbott B., *Antitrust Law Developments*, 3rd edn, vol. 1, American Bar Association, 1992.

Trachtenberg, Jeffrey A., *The Rain on Macy's Parade*, Crown Publishing Group, 1996.

Verloop, Peter, *Merger Control in the EU*, 3rd edn, Kluwer Law Intl, 1999.

Vlasic, Bill & Stertz, Bradley A., *Taken for a Ride: how DaimlerBenz drove off with Chrysler*, William Morrow & Co, 2001.

Wall, Joseph Frazier, *Andrew Carnegie*, University of Pittsburgh Press, 1989.

Wall, Stephen J. & Wall, Shannon Rye, *The Morning After: making corporate mergers work after the deal is sealed*, Perseus Books Group, 2000.

Wallace, James, *Overdrive: Bill Gates and the race to control cyberspace*, John Wiley & Sons, 1997.

Wasserstein, Bruce, *Big Deal: mergers and acquisitions in the digital age*, Warner Books, Incorporated, 2001.

Wasserstein, Bruce, *Corporate Finance Law: a guide for the executive*, McGraw-Hill, 1978.

Weidenbaum, Murray & Chilton, Kenneth, *Public Policy Toward Corporate Takeovers*, Transaction Books, 1988.

Wendel, Charles B., *The New Financiers: profiles of the leaders who are reshaping the financial services industry*, Irwin Professional Publications, 1996.

Woodhull, Nancy J. & Snyder, Robert W., *Media Mergers* (Media Studies Series), Transaction Publishers, 1997.

Yergin, Dantel, *The Prize: the epic quest for oil, money and power*, Simon & Schuster, 1991.

PUBLICATIONS AND WEBSITES

www.realcorporatelawyer.com (corporate and securities research)

www.ceoexpress.com (market news, stocks, and links to business research)

www.fedworld.gov (searchable information network of government sites and reports)

www.sec.gov (US Securities and Exchange Commission site)

www.ftc.gov (US Federal Trade Commission site)

www.nyse.com (information and statistics on all NYSE listed companies) www.business.com. (search engine, under financial services and investment banking and brokerage)

www.bizology.com. (information on buying and selling small businesses)

www.gecfo.com (explanation of different types of debt financing)

www.mergercentral.com (provides "MergerDay" – current accounts of M&A happenings, including "MergerMurmurs," inside look to deals and issues)

www.nvst.com. (mergers and acquisition instruction, includes the sale of books)

www.tfsd.com (provides M&A data and statistics)

www.business.gov (information and services the US government provides to businesses)

www.gsionline.com (includes customized search functions for filings of deals with specific features)

www.ft.com (*Financial Times* published)

www.wsj.com (*Wall Street Journal* published)

www.bloomberg.com (general information about worldwide financial markets)

www.redherring.com (information about technology and dot.coms)

www.tornado-insider.com (magazine for Europe's New Economy)

www.zephus.com (M&A database)

www.mergerstat.com (M&A transaction data, in-depth historical deal information)

ASSOCIATIONS

International Business Brokers
  Association (IBBA)
11250 Roger Bacon Drive
Suite 8
Reston, VA 20190
(703) 437–4377
www.bizmart.com/ibba

Association for Corporate
  Growth
1926 Waukegan Road
Suite 100
Glenview, IL 60025
(800) 699-1331
www.acg.org

International Merger and
   Acquisition Professionals
   (IMAP)
3232 Cobb Parkway
Suite 437
Atlanta, GA 30339
(770) 319-7797
www.imap.com

Directory of M&A Intermediaries
c/o The Buyout Directors
40 West 57th Street
11th Floor
New York, NY 10019
(212) 765-5311

MergerFACTS Monthly
c/o Securities Data Company
Two Gateway Center
Newark, NJ 07102
(201) 645-9609
ATTN: Leah Stack

American Society of Appraisers
   (ASA)
555 Herndon Parkway
Suite 125
Herndon, VA 20170
(800) 272-8258
www.appraisers.org

*Mergers & Acquisitions: The
   Dealmaker's Journal*
229 South 18th Street
Philadelphia, PA 19103
(215) 790-7000
ATTN: Martin Sikora, Editor

World M&A Network
c/o International Executive Reports
717 D Street, N.W.
Suite 300
Washington, DC 20004
(202) 628-7767
ATTN: John Bailey, Editor

Making it Work

Chapter 10 explains the ten steps or matters that companies should address in a business combination.

- » who handles business combination matters;
- » board and management consideration of potential business combinations;
- » ensuring that a company has adequate takeover defenses;
- » monitoring market activity;
- » remaining independent;
- » merger of equals;
- » joint ventures and strategic alliances;
- » sale of the company;
- » how to respond to informal and public offers; and
- » what is in a merger or acquisition contract.

The following are ten steps or matters that a company should keep in mind when addressing mergers and acquisitions. Some of these matters are important to address continuously. Some are pertinent when a particular merger or acquisition issue arises.

1. WHO HANDLES MERGERS AND ACQUISITIONS

Mergers and acquisitions are at the top of the list when it comes to companies considering their strategic plans. Since confidentiality is important, a company should task only a relatively small group of executive officers to consider and handle any issues that arise until a deal is announced publicly. These officers normally include the chief executive officer, chief operations officer, and chief financial officer, and perhaps include the general counsel and head of business development. As the likelihood of a deal increases, more officers may be consulted, after they have been reminded of the need for secrecy. Just before – and well after – a deal is announced, the company's investor relations, media relations, and legal department become critical participants in the transaction.

Quite a few outside consultants also are actively involved in helping companies consider their merger and acquisition alternatives. The company's investment banker and outside corporate lawyer are most useful in analyzing a deal and developing a strategic approach to it. As a result, they are intimately involved in the transaction and probably will make several formal presentations to the board of directors before the deal is complete. Once a deal is announced, the company relies on its public relations consultants and proxy solicitors to get the public to accept the deal and get the requisite shareholder vote.

2. MEDIA CONSIDERATIONS

Once a deal is announced, the company immediately is faced with many questions, from the media, investors, analysts, employees, customers, and the affected communities. Accordingly, the company must create presentations tailored for each of these groups. Some of the more important members of this group should be contacted personally and perhaps even a visit should be arranged. If a deal may be contested, this becomes even more important. This may include the larger institutional investors, primary analysts, journalists with the main-stream media, and even regulators if the deal may be challenged by the government. To be adequately prepared for a deal, companies should have standing procedures so that they can be quickly prepared to inform each of these groups when a deal is suddenly before them.

3. BOARD AND MANAGEMENT CONSIDERATIONS

As part of the planning process for mergers or acquisitions, a company must be prepared to act quickly – whether it be approached as a potential target or has a buying opportunity (which may be spurred by a competitor's approach to another competitor for which it wants to make an unsolicited bid). Frequent analysis of the fundamental financial picture of each potential target and acquiror must be conducted, either in-house or by a consultant.

The company's board should have the ability to convene a special board meeting at short notice. Potential business combinations should be routinely discussed at regular board meetings. At these meetings, the board should occasionally be briefed by M&A experts, including the company's investment bankers and outside lawyers, to assist them to remember what factors the board should be considering and educate directors about the current takeover activity. This also helps directors know the applicable law and familiarizes them with their advisors so that a trusting bond can be formed. As part of this ongoing discussion, hopefully the board will reach a consensus on what is the company's preferred strategic plan relating to mergers and acquisitions, whether it be a policy to remain independent and not engage in takeover discussions, or to be open to such discussions. In all cases, informed and full deliberation of merger and acquisition issues is critical to a director meeting its fiduciary duties.

For management, it may be helpful to hold periodic "fire drills" to test whether they are adequately prepared. These officers may want to keep a "warlist" to help them remember what they need to accomplish in various M&A scenarios. Management must ensure that each director knows that it should refer any approaches from a potential acquiror to the chief executive officer. Without this referral process, a company may unwittingly be placed into "play," partially because it was unprepared. In addition, the CEO should be the sole spokesperson for the company on merger and acquisition matters. This is important from a psychological standpoint and may be important from a legal perspective. In the US, companies are more likely not to run foul of the law if they have a policy of not commenting on takeover discussions and rumors and they abide by that policy.

4. TAKEOVER DEFENSES

The best preparation for an unexpected approach by a potential acquiror is to assume that one will occur. This assumption is not far fetched, particularly since unprepared companies are the most vulnerable to being approached since they lack the type of structural defenses that make takeovers so difficult. Without impediments from the company's charter, bylaws, and other major agreements, the premium necessary to conduct a takeover likely is lower and makes the company a more attractive target.

The company's investment banker and outside corporate lawyer play a key role in establishing these structural defenses. Firstly, they can help ensure that the company is incorporated in a jurisdiction that has laws that tend to protect incumbent management from ruining the company. In the US, companies are incorporated in one of the states and some states are known for their aggressive takeover laws. These laws allow companies to adopt protective measures in their charter and bylaws, as well as to establish roadblocks to unwanted acquisitions by mere operation of law. For example, these laws may include provisions to limit the activities of holders that quickly accumulate shares, ensure that a target receives a fair price, validate the use of poison pills, and allow companies to consider all their various constituencies when mulling an offer.

Some charter and bylaw provisions that protect companies are fairly standard. These include limiting the ability of stockholders to act by written consent and requiring them to provide advance notice of any proposals they seek to present to management at a stockholders' meeting. In addition, companies often limit the ability of stockholders to call a special meeting of stockholders; to remove directors without cause; and to expand the size of the board and fill vacancies. Some provisions have become less common in the face of opposition by institutional investors. These include staggered boards, supermajority voting requirements, cumulative voting, and preemptive rights.

Perhaps the most effective antitakeover device is the stockholder rights plan, also known as a poison pill. A poison pill gives a company's existing shareholders the right to acquire new shares of stock at significantly below-market prices upon the occurrence of triggering events related to an unsolicited takeover bid. The resulting dilution of the putative acquiror's interest would make proceeding with a bid without the target board's approval "financial suicide." Hence, the moniker "poison pill." Absent a shareholder approval requirement in a company's charter or bylaws, the board of directors may adopt a poison pill unilaterally.

Since their first use in the 1980s, they have been the subject of a number of lawsuits, particularly as investment bankers and lawyers have tried to make them more potent. For example, the ability to use so-called "dead-hand" poison pills was recently struck down in Delaware. A "dead-hand" provision allows only "continuing directors" to redeem (or approve the redemption of) the pill. Continuing directors are defined as the directors who were in office when the pill was adopted or directors who were endorsed by such directors. Thus, the definition of continuing directors excludes those elected to facilitate a transaction opposed by the incumbent board. Companies incorporated in other states also have dismantled this type of pill due to pressure from institutional investors.

Companies can build takeover protection into many other agreements that they have. These include structuring loan agreements, indentures and employee stock ownership plans. All compensatory arrangements can have an antitakeover component, including stock option plans and employment contracts. Many senior officers have their own severance arrangements, known as "golden parachutes," that can be quite expensive for an acquiror – and lucrative for management.

5. STRATEGIC PLANNING CONSIDERATIONS

Strategic planning for mergers and acquisitions involves common sense much like any other event. The first consideration should be whether a merger or acquisition is appropriate. Whether you are a buyer or seller, an analysis should be conducted regarding:

» the strengths and weaknesses of your company;
» the potential opportunities for acquisitions; and
» other alternatives to an acquisition.

Secondly, the choice of an appropriate candidate for a merger or acquisition will weigh heavily in making such a transaction a success, both financially and operationally. Begin looking for potential partners, thereby creating options. Understand the time commitment it takes to put together a successful transaction. Thirdly, if you are a seller, conduct a legal audit of your organization. This means taking steps to prepare the company for sale from a corporate housekeeping perspective and anticipating questions and concerns of a prospective buyer. Then, get the company ready for the buyer's due diligence investigation. The goal is to find any issues before the buyer does, and to get as many issues corrected before the process begins.

6. DUE DILIGENCE IN THE MERGER AND ACQUISITION PROCESS

The due diligence process is critical to determine whether to enter into a merger or acquisition – and not performing adequate due diligence is a classic mistake. The lawyers and accountants perform the due diligence investigation. Generally, it is conducted principally on the seller. However, if the buyer is using stock consideration, the seller may also perform due diligence on the buyer. The due diligence process involves a legal, financial, and strategic review of all the seller's documents, contracted relationships, operating history, and organizational structure. Due diligence is not just a process, it is also a reality check – a test of whether the factors driving the deal and making it look attractive to the parties are real or illusory.

In a due diligence investigation, lawyers and accountants pore over the official internal books and records of the other party to the deal, verifying, checking the accuracy of the factual representations, and looking for red flags. They may be assisted by other experts, such as environmental consultants and real estate appraisers. Effective due diligence is both an art and a science. The art is the style and experience to know which questions to ask and how and when to ask them. The science is in the preparation of comprehensive and customized checklists. The best way for the buyer to ensure that virtually no stone remains unturned is effective preparation and planning. When done properly, due diligence is performed in multiple stages. Firstly, all the basic data is gathered and specific topics are identified. Follow-up questions and additional data gathering can be performed in subsequent rounds of diligence.

7. REGULATORY CONSIDERATIONS

There is a wide variety of regulatory considerations in a merger or acquisition, usually falling into one of two categories: (1) general regulatory issues, which affect all types of transactions; and (2) industry-specific regulatory issues, which affect only certain types of transactions in certain industries. The general regulatory considerations include issues such as antitrust, environmental, securities, and employee benefit matters. Some industry-specific regulatory issues involve federal and state regulators which may exercise rights of approval over those transactions that involve a change in ownership or control or that have an anticompetitive effect on a given industry.

Any transaction in the broadcasting, health care, insurance, public utilities, transportation, telecommunications, financial services, and even the defense contracting industries should be analyzed carefully to determine what level of governmental approval may be necessary to close the transaction. Regulatory issues can cause the success or failure of deals. For example, in the summer of 2001, the European Union rejected the much publicized proposed GE-Honeywell merger which had an estimated value of $42 billion. The European regulators effectively killed the deal when they demanded that GE make divestitures. This regulatory action cost these companies not only time and money but prestige and reputation.

The regulatory component of mergers and acquisitions must be thought through in detail prior to entering into a transaction. Sometimes it is merely preparing perfunctory applications. However, other times it can involve governmental hearings that may determine the life or death of the transaction. At the very least, the regulatory process must be factored into the amount of time it will take to accomplish the transaction. The more time spent analyzing regulatory issues at the beginning of the transaction, the smoother the transaction will proceed.

8. STRUCTURING AND PRICING THE DEAL

There are virtually any number of ways in which a corporate merger or acquisition may be structured. Indeed, there are probably as many potential deal structures as there are qualified and creative transactional lawyers and investment bankers. The goal is not to create the most complex structure, but rather one that reflects the goals and objectives of the buyer and seller. Naturally, not all of the objectives of each party will be met each time; there will almost always be a degree of negotiation and compromise. But virtually all structures, even the most complex, are at their roots basically either mergers or acquisitions, including the purchase or consolidation of either stock or assets. The creativity often comes in structuring the deal to achieve a particular tax advantage or strategic result or to accommodate a multi-step or multi-party transaction.

There are a wide variety of corporate, tax, and securities law issues that help decide the structure of a given transaction; however, at the heart of the various structured alternatives is the form of compensation that will be paid. The method of payment for the acquisition of stock or assets ordinarily involves balancing both the business and tax considerations. The form of payment generally includes some component of cash and securities. In a stock swap, the most difficult aspect is determining the value of the consideration during the pendency of the transaction because the price of the buyer's stock will fluctuate.

In a given merger or acquisition, there is a wide variety of tax and accounting issues that must be considered and understood as part of the negotiation and structuring of the transaction. These affect the valuation and pricing, as well as the structure of the deal, and may be a condition to the closing. Mergers and acquisitions may be completely tax free, partially tax free, or entirely taxable to the seller. Each party and its advisers will have its own often differing view on how the transaction should be structured from a tax perspective, depending on the non-tax strategic objectives of both parties and their respective tax and financial positions.

9. POST-CLOSING CONSIDERATIONS

Although the focus in a merger or acquisition transaction is the closing, the buyer needs to be mindful that the closing of the transaction is really only the beginning. The success or failure of a transaction will depend largely on the buyer's ability to integrate the two companies. The integration of human resources, the corporate cultures, the operating and management information systems, the accounting methods and financial practices, and related matters are often the most difficult part of completing a merger or acquisition. The consequences of a rocky transition will be the buyer's inability to realize the true value of the transaction, wasted time and resources devoted to solving post-closing problems, and in some cases even litigation. The buyer must have a procedure in place in order to deal effectively with the transitional integration issues and must demonstrate leadership to implement its procedures.

10. ESTABLISHING A TIME FRAME

Because of the considerations that must be taken into account and the number of parties required to accomplish a merger or acquisition, it is essential that a time and responsibilities schedule is prepared at the outset of the transaction. A merger and acquisition may take anywhere from a couple of weeks to more than a year, depending on the complexity of the transaction. As a result, the items to be accomplished and the person responsible for such items need to be set forth on a checklist. This type of schedule will allow the transaction to run smoothly and allow the company's management to monitor the progress. The schedule should also be revisited continuously during the process and updated when and if necessary.

Overall, the due diligence process, when done properly, can be tedious, frustrating, time-consuming and expensive. Yet it is a necessary prerequisite to a well-planned acquisition, and it can be quite informative and revealing in its analysis of the target company and its measure of the costs and risks associated with the transaction. Buyers should expect sellers to become defensive and impatient during the due diligence process.

Frequently asked Questions (FAQs)

Q1: How many mergers and acquisitions occurred during the frenetic pace of the 1990s?

A: See Chapter 1: Introductory comments.

Q2: How are various transactions structured to meet the objectives of the acquiror and the target company?

A: See Chapter 2: What is a Merger or Acquisition?

Q3: What are the origins of the modern hostile takeover?

A: See Chapter 3. Evolution of Merger and Acquisition Activity.

Q4: How can companies use acquisitions to gain technology necessary to stay competitive in their industry?

A: See Chapter 4. The E-Dimension: Impact of the Internet and Other New Technologies.

Q5: What should an acquiror consider before approaching a company located in another country about a merger?

A: See Chapter 5. Global Mergers and Acquisitions.

Q6: What funds might be available to management to conduct a leveraged buy-out?

A: See Chapter 6. State of the Art.

Q7: What governmental and cultural factors affect M&A activity in Europe, the US, and Japan?

A: See Chapter 7: In Practice: M&A Success Stories.

Q8: Where can I find definitions of the basic M&A terms?

A: See Chapter 8: Glossary.

Q9: Where can I find the seminal books, useful publications, Websites, treaties, and associations for understanding M&A?

A: See Chapter 9: Resources.

Q10: What are the issues that must be addressed in a business combination?

A: See Chapter 10: Ten Steps to Handling a Merger or Acquisition.

Index

Printed and bound in the UK by
CPI Antony Rowe, Eastbourne

Printed and bound by CPI Group (UK) Ltd, Croydon, CR0 4YY

29/11/2023

08198393-0001